Mimicking Nature

Mimicking Nature
A solution for Sustainable Development

Ashokan Kannarath
M.Sc, P.hD, B.Ed, D.I.T, I.P.B.I, M.Biol (S.L)

*After decades of faithful
study, ecologists have begun
to fathom hidden likenesses
among many interwoven
systems. . . . a canon of nature's
laws, strategies, and
principles . . .
Nature runs on sunlight.
Nature uses only the energy
it needs.
Nature fits form to function.
Nature recycles everything.
Nature rewards
cooperation.
Nature banks on diversity.
Nature demands local
expertise.
Nature curbs excesses from
within.
Nature taps the power of
limits.*

**Janine M. Benyus
(Founder of Biomimcry Institute)**

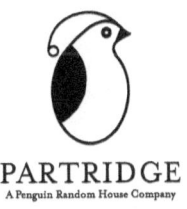

PARTRIDGE
A Penguin Random House Company

To order additional copies of this book, contact
Partridge India
000 800 10062 62
www.partridgepublishing.com/india
orders.india@partridgepublishing.com

CONTENTS

PREFACE

Biomimicry or biomimetics is one of the latest, fast developing branches in biology. It is the application of natural, biological secret of living things for the betterment of human kind. Nature keeps or tries to do everything in a balanced state. A slight change in this balance may leads to vulnerability ranging from slight ecological imbalance to major ecological backlashes that we cannot repair in the future. Identification, exploitation of nature's secret is not a new concept. Man used the secret of nature for his well being right from the beginning of mankind. Tribal know the secret of the nature better than others, because tribal are part and parcel of nature in its true sense. Use of poison spread arrow for hunting by tribal world over is well known fact. Use of various natural herbal remedies by our Rushies (saints) and saints since time immemorial is a kind of biomimicry. People who lived in the forest know by practice that some of the plants are non-palatable to cattle, hence they used cattle to know the poison or dangerous chemicals present in some plants, which may be fatal. Differentiation of poisonous mushroom form non-poisonous and extraction of mushroom poison for the treatment of leprosy is one kind of biomimicry. Trapping of prey by spiders by its own sticky net is the inspiration for making many fly traps and even the preparation of various net used now a days. Changing the colour to protect some animals from its enemy is the inspiration for camouflage technique used by military regiments during intercontinental war. Injection of poison by honey bees, scorpion and other such creatures may be the inspiration for the construction of latest syringe. Thus biomimcry is the technique of copying the nature. The term biomimcry or biomimetics is derived from Greek words bios, meaning life, and mimesis, meaning to imitate. If apply the principles and secret of nature for our development both technological and cultural, the nature will preserve its biodiversity and consequently the integrity and sustainable development will result. Our ecosystem is in great danger than ever since the birth of earth. Day by day the earth's integrity become deteriorate and if the trends of today continue a day will come "Earth's resources" become the rarest things in the universe. There comes the value of sustainable development. Nature prepares and applies very sophisticated materials under low temperature with least pollution. For example marine muscle synthesis glue to stick on rocks or other substrates under low temperature with least pollution that works in water without any fault. There is no man made known material that works such a precision as the byssian thread glue. The light emitted by fire fly is another good example of how nature works without causing their integrity. To day by applying the principle of nature man made a lot of things right from the zip-fastener to sophisticated robots. All these developments will goes to the ardent workers in the field of biomimicry. To mention a few is Jack Steele, who coined the term "biomimicry", Martin Caidin, he introduced jack Steele and his works in his novel "Cybor" which later aired as "The six Million Dollar man" as a T.V serial. The term was later popularized by Janine Benyus. The role of Janine Benyus in the field of biomimcry is amazing and she awarded many prestigious awards in the field of sustainable development and biomimicry. In her 1997 book "Biomimcry: Innovation Inspired by Nature she defined biomimcry as a "New science that studies nature's models and then imitates or takes inspiration from these designs and processes to solve problems".

Biomimcry is a very promising science which teaches us how to fulfill the modern man's requirements in eco-friendly manner. Biomimicry teaches us how to construct eco-friendly city, robots, signal lights, design boards, nano-tubes, bullet proof jackets and many more, that also without causing any pollution and using least expenditure. Let us hope that this branch will save us from the ever growing menace and fear of the existence of the Mother Earth.

This book is specially designed to get a basic idea about sustainable development, how animal and plant models become an ideal natural teacher to construct and design modern man's requirements without causing pollution. This book has nine chapters, the first section is devoted for introduction, the second for sustainable development, the third one for inspiration derived from plants, fourth one for inspiration derived from animals, the fifth chapter is devoted for research in biomimicry and sixth chapter is for development in biomimcry at molecular level, the seventh one is for modern city planning with special reference to LAVASA in India, the eighth chapter is for explain some case studies in biomimcry and the last chapter is to know the reader about some access point in biomimcry resources, followed by further study and as a last section is the index to the contents.

The third chapter dedicated to innovation inspired by plant kingdom is organized with 24 examples from plants including algae, bryophytes, pteridophytes, gymnosperms and angiosperms. This chapter is also included some inspiration from bacteria and fungi.

The fourth chapter for the animal inspiration in biomimcry explained about 35 animals belongs to various phyla and their innovative ideas. Biomimcry research explains various research aspects of spider silk and mussel adhesive. The seventh chapter explained about LAVASA the modern two planning which mimics natures law for sustainable development in an elegant manner with many photographs.

Let us hope that the book will pave the way for diverting the thought process towards the sustainable development while doing anything with the expenditure out of nature's resources. This type of study is essentially necessary for the long lasting existence of our Mother Earth for our won purpose and for the coming generations in existing from.

CHAPTER-1

Introduction

Nature, the source everything, provides us a lot of ideas and products, man exploit this since his origin. The prehistoric human ancestors like tree shrews and its siblings made an evolutionary sojourn to reach the modern man. The steps followed by these prehistoric human creatures baptized as human evolution. The driving force of this evolution is the timely need to live successfully in the surroundings. He is very helpless in front of wild animals, but his brain power is dominant in thinking process than any organisms in the nature. His power of thinking and discrimination make him unique from other organisms. When plunged into the grass root reason for human evolution we can find that human evolution is the evolution of his power to copy nature's secret in one or other way to live successfully in nature. Natural selection of his physical and mental ability is unpredictable that within a short period of time he becomes the master of the world. But, according to Leonardo Da *Vinci* "Human ingenuity may make various inventions, but it will never devise any inventions more beautiful, nor more simple, nor more to the purpose than Nature does; because in her inventions nothing is wanting and nothing is superfluous". In the words of Aristotle, "If one way be better than another, that you may be sure it is Nature's way". Really speaking our ancestors are best researchers. He finds out millions of plant materials that can assist him in one way or other. All these happened only by his trial and error in copying nature's secret, an inborn behavior. The flying bird inspired Wright Brothers to invent aero plan. The leaf of giant Amazon water-lily inspired Joseph Paxton to designs not only for the glass-houses at Chatsworth but also, a few years later, for his architectural masterpiece, the Crystal Palace in London. The human femur bone balances our body weight. The network like structure in the anatomy of human femur bone which both allows for circulation as well as strength inspired the architect of the Eiffel Tower. Hooks on burrs and other seeds Velcro, zip-fastener. Conch shell nacre (mother of pearl coating) and Abalone consists of alternating layers of soft and hard material so mechanic al shocks in the strong part are absorbed by the soft. This inspired to produce the bodies of vehicles or like one that needs to be weightless or lightweight but crack—resistant. An ideal example for this kind of natures activity is network repair systems in ant colony i.e. when accidently the ant colony is destructed, ants can find a new suitable site and transfer resources effectively and with least energy consumption inspired I. T industries and computer technologists are studying this model to analyze damaged computers and programs in systems and quickly resolve to prevent computer crashes. Hence this type of structures self-assembles and repairs automatically. Teeth, bones, shells of antlers, inspired for CAD technology and ink-jet. The secret of sealing by barnacle valve inspired plumbers and help for heart surgeons alike. Blue mussel adhesive, Bat and marine mammal navigation, Blue mussel byssus (The tether attaching the mussel to a solid surface), Blue mussel byssus sealant, Camouflaging Cephalopods, Cell membranes, Chlorophyll and enzymes, Cockroach cuticle, Crab shell, Crocodile Skin, Cyanobacteria, Dolphin and shark skin, Narwhal tusk, Elastin, the elastic protein in heart muscle, the biogeochemical cycles, Filter feeders, Fish antifreeze, Fly ear drums, Food webs, Forests, Forest Floor, Fruits and Vegetables, Fungi, Gecko toes, Hibernating bears, Horses Teeth, House Fly, Human tongue and ear drum, Hummingbirds, Iridescent feathers and butterfly wings, Jewel Beetle, Kelp, Lemurs and many other primates, Lobster, Mangroves, and other marsh plants, Mantled howler monkeys, Marshes, Microtubules, Namibian Beetles, Redwood Trees/ Western Hemlock, Native grazers, Natural disturbance, Natural selection, Nautilus shell, lily bud unfurling, human pore, water down a drain, Neurons and other kinds of cells, Penguin insulation, Porcupine quills, Prairie dog burrows, Rhinoceros horn, Sea Cucumbers, Sharks, anemones, and other marine creatures, Slug mucous, Snake Fangs, Sphinx moth, Sponges, Tuna, Venomous snakes, Vulture wings, Whale Blubber, Whale tubicles, Woodpecker and many more are wonderful examples to be explained, but let us wait for a while. The habit of copying secret of nature leads to molecular level also. Thus a new branch in science is formed, "Nanotechnology". The main difference between man-made materials and nature products are, the latter is degradable, requires no sophisticated technology, not required high temperature and are not causing any kind of environmental pollution. A spider constructing web under such a condition and each fiber is five times stronger than steel. The inner shell of abalone is twice as resistant as the ceramics that even advanced technology can produce. The adhesive that mussel uses to moor themselves to rocks maintains its properties even under water. No human technology so far developed to make such glue or materials under water or low temperature that also without causing any pollution. The properties of materials prepared by nature are harder, stronger, and more resistant and have superior physical, mechanical, chemical and electromagnetic properties, possess lightness and the ability to withstand high temperature required by vehicles as rockets, space shuttles and the satellites etc. the philosopher Eric Hoffer once wrote "Nature is a self-made machine, more perfectly automated than any automated machine. To create something in the image of nature is to create a machine and it was by learning the inner working of nature that man became a builder of machines". Man copied everything from nature. The various things copied from nature leads him to the modern world. The simple self-protecting equipment like harpoon and arrow is the product of inspiration copied from the usage of horns by animals to protect itself. Even the nanotechnology is the development of inspiration drawn from nature. Human, the most intelligent product evolution not only copied the secret of nature, but he also synthesized his own materials independent of nature. All such materials are produced against the laws of nature. Hence, in the course of time it became a burden and caused ecological backlashes of unpredictable. All organisms including plants, animals, fungi, algae and bacteria must grow, maintain, feed and reproduce to ensure their short-term and long-term sustainability. The same can be said for human. But the way industrial humans have gone about for meeting their needs is quite different from the way other organisms survive, and therein lies the root of our sustainability crisis. Non-human organisms, by and large, meet their basic life requisites within the confines and constraints of their environment. Within that habitat context, they adapt, migrate, or go extinct. Adaptations, both behavioral and physiological, help sustain individuals in the short-term, and ultimately lead to genetic adaptations that sustain the species in the long-term over the last 3.8 billion years; these adaptations have led to the evolution of 30 million species each with its own unique way of meeting its needs in harmony with its environment. Ecologists have long been intrigued by how complex, efficient, and effective these adaptations are. Despite their immense variety natural system from microscopic amoeba to entire ecosystem and biomass share at least one trait. They are limited in their adaptations by the constraints of their environment and natural laws of biology. Sustainable business strategies have previously focused on making industries more efficient such as using less waste, less energy, less material. This is an important first step, but without system change, it can still lead to deteriorating natural systems. Old-economy 'treatment' industries (e.g. waste management, potable water supply, etc.) have attempted to mitigate and manage the pollution and waste as an 'end of pipe' approach to system deterioration, but engineers and designers are now realizing that this is not a sustainable approach. Consider that for the majority of our time on the planet as a species, we have been hunters and gatherers. As hunters and gatherers (*harvesting nature*) and then as agrarians through pre-industrial times (*harnessing nature*), we paid a great deal of attention to natural systems as a source of knowledge, as Janine Benyus puts it, '*we naturally mimicked the organisms that we admired*'. As our knowledge of natural systems increased, we began to harness those organisms that we needed, then to process nature's raw materials to produce products and services (for example through agricultural practices, and steel and plastics manufacturing). Once we realized that we could make value-added products from nature's raw resources, we began paying less attention to natural systems, seeing them more as a source of inputs for our products and services. As we transitioned from organism domestication to mass production and industrialization we adopted the mindset of 'animal as factory'. Today, when we try to address problems arising from old-economy technologies (such as filtration, adhesion, desalination, energy harvesting), we tend to study the way humans have problem-solved, rather than looking to nature for advice. However, combining our knowledge of processes with our knowledge of natural systems, we now have the opportunity to build products and services that are in harmony with natural systems, we can create 'Biomimetic' solutions. When we view nature as a source of advice rather than goods, the rationale for protecting wild species and their habitats also becomes self-evident.

In our country, India, the indiscriminate use of plastics in varied forms like milk bags to refrigerator packing and consequent waste spreading thousands acres of land mass is a serious problem in front of both government and human sustainability. We should rethink about the degradable materials for packing purpose. Nature in their packing technique use degradable things like cuticle, cellulose, chitin, hemi cellulose, pectin, silk fibers, shell of calcium carbonate, silica, fibers etc. All these natural packing materials are synthesized under low temperature, with minimum cost, maximum duration and biodegradable. Therefore it never causes any kind of pollution and after the use it becomes the part of the nature by recycling. Man-made packing materials are synthetic, non-degradable, costly, and causes many kind of pollutions. Every bag that's washed down a drain during rainfall ends up in the sea every bag that's flushed down a toilet (many mall bags are), ends up in the sea—every bag that's blown into a river will most likely end up in the sea. Besides choking drains, plastics are highly toxics. When burned they release cancer-causing gases. Lying in the garbage, polythene bags also find their way in gut of cattle, asphyxiating the animals. The cheap bags contain chemicals such as cadmium—or lead—based chemicals that are harmful to health. They leach into vegetables, meat and food. About 100,000 animals such as dolphins, turtle whales, penguins are killed every year due to plastic bags. Many animals ingest plastic bags, mistaking them for food, and therefore die. And worse, the ingested plastic bag remains intact even after the death and decomposition of the animal. Thus, it lies around in the landscape where another victim may ingest it. Thus the concept of biomimcry should reach to the common people the earliest is a must for the sustainability of human being.

This book aims to introduce the concept of biomimcry, sustainability development, how to learn from plants and animals the secret of sustainability and many examples from the plants and animals for biomimcry. This book is very useful to all the beginners who interested in biomimcry and really thinking about the sustainable development for the existence of human kind and preservation of natural resources for the coming generations. It also devoted a complete chapter to validate the first "biomimicking city" in India the LAVAS

CHAPTER-2

Sustainable Development: A Global Issue

The concept of sustainable development arouses from various ecological—environmental initiations in the last few decades and was defined in 1987 by world commission on Environment and development as "Development that meets the needs of the present without compromising the ability of future generations to meet their own needs". This definition clearly indicates that sustainable development encompasses number of interrelated branches of study like environmental itself, economics, social and health within the constraints of natural resources. It warns al the categories of people, be aware the development of any kind should not cause the exploitation of the natural buffer stocks. Development should be happen by forecasting the need of the coming generation to be fulfilled and should not be starved for anything. In this chapter we can analyze the various kinds of development-economical, social and cultural on the background of sustainable development.

Poverty reduction

Poverty and inequality among mankind is a common phenomenon in both developed and developing countries. The gap between poor and rich is unpredictably increased in developing nation. Reduction of this inequality is the aim of any government and ruling section. The international community MDGs (Millennium development Goals) is working to achieve halving the poor by 2015. The criterion for this poverty is those getting daily wages less than one dollar. This agency also supports the developing countries to achieve the goal. This community also aims to promote gender equality and empowering women as effective ways to combat poverty, hunger and disease. To reduce inequality and reduction of poverty private sector can do much. Industries provide job opportunities, promote business investment, foster technological upgrading and dynamism, and improve human skills and create skilled jobs, and through inter-sectorial linkages establish the foundation for both agriculture and services to expand. All these contribute to increase the daily earning of the pro-poor and help to alleviate the condition of poor and establish better standard of the poor section.

Government should take appropriate steps to increase the income of the poor section by promoting small scale industries, subsidizing farming and farm management, sanctioning loans to maintain cattle breed, starting new farm practices, an industries like fish culturing, apiculture, poultry, and so and so. UNIDO will support the poor nation to build up small scale industries. Collaboration to agencies like UNIDO will assists to link domestic enterprises to international investment and technology flows and it will help to access resources and support services that small and medium enterprises require to become more competitive. Competition, innovation and entrepreneurships are basic sources productivity growth. Along with these resources a proper planning and incentive structure will definitely help us to produce more sustainable jobs and affordable goods and services. Inspiration to small scale and medium scale industries are not only productive but also improve the pro-poverty in developing nations, a dream of Mahatma Gandhi. Even after many decades of mahatma's death the policy and programs laid by him is inevitable to the modern society who runs behind high-tech in developing countries. The SMEs not only reduce the poverty but also encourage sustainable development. Inspiration of business like silkworm culture, apiculture is not only beneficial financially but also beneficial to the nature due to its sustainable attitude.

Globalization of trade

Globalization of trade is one of the most needed requirements for the economic growth of a nation. Entering in global trade make an entrepreneur more efficient in trade and get better value for the products which was previously masked the local trading markets. This aspect of the trade not only forces the manufacturer to produce high quality products but also the quality required by the markets. Thus the globalization force the traders to later ones products according to the need of the society. If the product is harmful concerned with health and environmental view it should be changed so that it must reduce pollution and encourage sustainable development. UNIDO (United Nations Industrial Development Organization). This organization promotes industrial development for poverty reduction, inclusive globalization and environmental sustainability. The main aim of the UNIDO is to promote and accelerates sustainable industrial development in developing countries. UNIDO provides technical supports and implements various projects. Poverty reduction is another. Not secondary, aim of UNIDO in developing countries. UNIDO also support to achieve standards regarding food hygiene and food safety (ISO 22000), quality management (ISO 14001) and social accountability (SA 8000). When we are talking about sustainable trade then biomimicry become a priority aspects. Because biomimcry produce the trade materials by copying the secret of the nature, that itself is sustainable way.

Energy and environment

The production of industrial commodities and its consumption is overridden the renewable capacity of the natural resources and the capacity of the authorities to mange pollution directly or indirectly and immediately or long lasting nature. Industrial growth definitely improved the living standard of the poor especially in the urban area, but people residing in the rural area remain at the same bottom line of the poverty. A balanced pace in the development of industry, poverty reduction and growth of the urban area is a need for the sustainable development in the future. Global climate change is another serious problem facing by developing countries, especially least developing countries (LDCs), many of which are inadequate in compacting the ever increasing pollution and the sufferer is not only the country itself but also globally. This change in climate may leads to desertification, rise in sea level, severe weather events and shortage of fresh water, which in turn cause cross border conflict and uncontrollable migration. UNIDO understand the back lash of this type of industrial development and forced to eco-friendly products which is more degradable and sustainable. Product alteration and machinery alteration may help us to achieve this goal to an extent. Some data regarding the poverty status of the global scenario is given below.

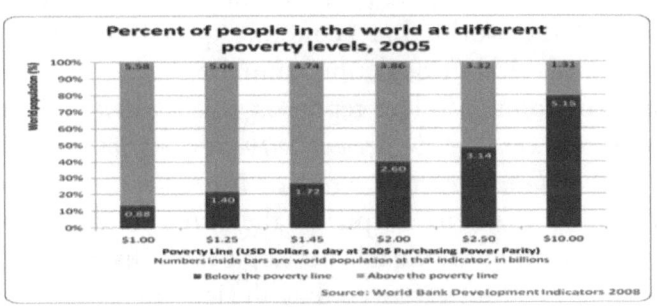

Share of world's private consumption, 2005

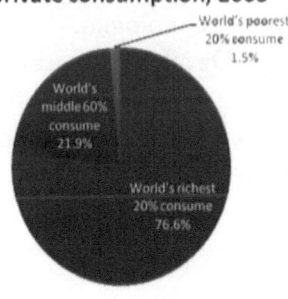

Source: World Bank Development Indicators 2008

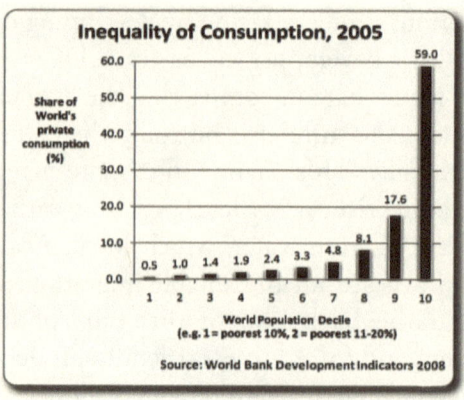

Summit on sustainable development

Brundtland report (Our common future) in 1987 alerted the world that economic growth should be sustained without depleting natural resources or harm the environment. The report *says "Development that meets the needs of the present without compromising the ability of future generation to meet their own needs"*. The Brundtland report emphasis the three fundamental components of sustainable development—environment, economy and society. According the report:-

Environment: We should conserve and enhance our resources base, by gradually changing the ways in which we develop and use technologies.

Social equity: Developing nation must be allowed to meet their basic needs of employment, food, energy, water and sanitation. If this is to be done in sustainable manner, then there is a definite need for a sustainable level of population.

Economic growth: Economic growth should be revived and developing nations should be allowed a growth of equal quality to the developed nations.

To assess the achievement by Brundtland report Rio earth summit was organized in 1992 at Rio de Janeiro in Brazil. The Rio summit produced a number of outcomes including:

1. The convention on Biological Diversity:
2. The frame work convention on climate change:
3. Principles of forest management:
4. Agenda 21:

The convention on biodiversity

Identify the components of biodiversity that are useful in conservation. These components must then be used sustainably and activities that may harm the diversity must be monitored.

1. Develop national strategies for the conservation and sustainable use of biodiversity.
2. Integrate conservation and sustainable use of biodiversity into planning and policy making.
3. Help people understand the importance of planning and policy making by using the media and educational programmes.
4. Establish laws to protect and conserve threatened species and protected areas. Around these areas, environmentally sound development must be used.
5. Restore degraded ecosystem and promote the recovery of threatened species.

6. Establish ways to control the risk from organisms modified by biotechnology.
7. Use the participation of members of the public within projects that threaten biodiversity.

Economic value on environment

Putting economic value on environment is a dedicated work to keep the sustainable development of the nature for the future generation. We have inborn tendency of extracting anything from the nature without thinking the ecological backlashes in the future. Nature's resources are free and can exploit any one without any objection. But bear in mind that future is fate of the earth and we have to preserve it for our coming generations. Millennium Ecosystem assessment shows that nearly $2/3^{rd}$ of the natural resources are in declining phase world over (Pierce, 2002). Extinction rate of our biodiversity is in alarming condition. Near about 50% of our natural resources and living organisms are vanished from the earth's laps. Naturally the question arise why do depleting our natural wealth even though it is an essential part to sustain the man hood?. The main reason behind this indiscriminate use of nature is it is free and cost we have to pay for. But in real sense the cost we have to pay for this barbarous use of the nature is unpredictable. The ever increasing CO2 and consequently global warming and unpredictable consequence that we face today in the form of different types of diseases, flood, earthquake an even the tsunami all these are the consequence of indiscriminate use of the natural resources. Thus we should protect the nature at any cost. Environmental report card, pollution penalty, common property right, cost-benefit analysis, defining property right for pollution are some of the measures to be implemented to reduce the over exploitation of natural resources.

Chapter-3

Inspiration derived from Plant kingdom

Plant kingdom inspired people from common man to world famous scientists alike, and made a lot of things useful to common man and in sophisticated scientific machineries. To mention a few is the common zip-fastener on one hand to robotic machine to other end. Many kinds of local and scientifically proven medicines are product from plants which inspired to produce many analogues. This topic is dedicated to explore the various things, energy and concepts derived or inspired by plants or part thereof or idea from plant behavior. The aim of this chapter is to introduce the concept of biomimcry and its palliation by deriving idea from plants. Let me explain the secret derived from plants one by one.

VELCRO

One of the most famous and pioneer example for biomimcry is the Velcro zip fastener. Velcro is a USA based company producing a wide variety of products like loop fastener and hook fastener, adhesives, for disposable application it produce no-woven loop materials, EVAPTEX fabric-a moisture wicking, breathing and durable knit, electrical system, flame maintained products, fire retardant hooks, flex-Zone diaper tabs, health and beauty and high technology hooks. It now established in eleven countries like Australia, Canada, Caribbean, China, France, Germany, Italy, Mexico, South and Central America, Spain and United Kingdom. The Velcro branded Fastener was invented by a Swiss, Commugny, Electrical Engineer, George de Mestral in 1941 (Mc Sweeney et al; 1999Stephen, 2007).

History of the discovery

Mestral once on return from morning walk with his dog in the Alps, he noticed that the dogs' fur was fastened some seeds and so his trousers. A close observation reveled that it was the seeds of burdock. Burdock is a plant belongs to the genus *Arcticum*. It is a biennial plant of family Asteraceae

He examined the seeds under the microscope and observed that the seed was provided with hundreds of tiny "hooks". The hooks can catch on anything with a loop i.e. clothing, hair, or animal fur etc. He consults many experts in this field but the result was simple insult. He managed to contact with a weaver and prepared something like this opposite hooks on threads but it was not successful for further reproduction due to its resistant to friction. So thought of some nylon materials because nylon is does not break easily, rot or attack by fungus and we can produce nylon thread with desired thickness. To make hooks on the nylon thread was very tedious to him. So he just plans to give up his idea. But suddenly ho got an idea of trim the hooks on shears and make hooks that will match up exactly with loops in the pile. Further eight ears lapsed to mechanize the product. And after two more ears it become perfectly mechanized and prepared the zip-fattener what we see today. He submitted this work for patency in Switzerland in 1951. This patent was granted in 1955 by Swiss government. After a few years he got the patent and open shops in Germany, Great Britain, Italy, Switzerland, Netherland, Canada and Belgium. He spread the antenna to Manchester and New Hampshire in USA. Sylkvia Porter he obtained patent in many country. Now it is used in aerospace to help astronauts to prepare space suits, scuba and marine gear. Alter NASA adopted it and its fame doubled within a few years. Today, more than 300 trademarks in about 159 countries following Mistral's idea.

Lotus effect

Nilembo nicufera, commonly known as lotus, sacred lotus, Indian lotus belong the family Niumbonaceae. It is an aquatic perennial plant. Its seeds remain under favorable condition for many years (Miller *et al*, 2002). It grows in freshwater bodies. The attracting feature of this plant is that its leaves are dirt free throughout the year even in dirtiest environment. When water rolling over the leaves the water drops collect the dirt and makes the surface dirt free. This common observation prompts two botanists in the University of Bonn, Barthlott and Neinhuis, in 1975 to study more about its cleaning secret. Previously it was thought that the clean surface is due to its smooth surface itself. The study of these two botanists by using electron microscope revealed that the surface of the leaf is fabricated in such a way that no dirt will adhere on it. Even though the surface of the lotus leaf appears smooth on gross observation, under the high power microscope it showed many nano-ridges and groves and give rough surface appearance. A physical explanation for the dirt free surface of lotus came due to two facts, one is the nano-projection form the surface itself and other is its hydrophobic nature due to waxy coating, so remain badly wet able. This nano structure and less wet able property of the surface of the lotus leaf prompt Barthlott and Neinhuis to give the name "LOTU EFFECT

Innovation form Lady's mantle plant leaf

It is an ideal plant to explain the secret of lotus effect. The surface of the mantle plant leaf is covered with tiny, cuticular waxy dandruff which is elastic and hydrophilic hair clusters. These hairs protect the leaf from accumulation of dirt. When water come in contact with these tiny waxy hairs rolled up and from droplets. These water droplets then pushed on the tip of the hairs because the tips are more hydrophilic than the base (Otten, 2003). The interesting observation is that the contact angle of the droplet meniscus at the hair is below 60° all along the hair. The advancing contact angle along the hair is also not larger than 60°. This property suck the liquid into the hair as blotting paper do. The water drop when in contact with cuticle is about 90° and turn to droplet of 60° on contact with tiny, waxy hairs and advantage of being absorbed to the tip of the hair in the form of drops due to the more hydrophilicity of the tip. These drops when contact with other drop become the state of fiber wetting and aggregate into bigger one. This wetting mechanism is advantages to organism because hairs in animals assists in thermoregulation i.e. drawing in cool air when wet and retaining warmth when dry. More over this is renewable material and insulation, and it is biodegradable. This the secret of the lady mantle plant can be used to build envelope industry or self cleaning material producing industries, self paint industry, thermoregulation or HVAC engineering.

The surface cleaning secret lie in the facts that when the droplet rolling down the dirt is stick to the droplet due to high absorption (Cohesiver) force of the dirt to the droplet than on the surface. Thus the rolling off droplet collect the dirt and self cleaning the surface of leaves of plants like lady mantle, colcasia, lotus etc. This principle can be applied to commercial product like exterior and interior wall paints. So a simple wash or simply the rain fall on the wall clean the surface easily and no need to coat the wall year after year, an innovation inspired from nature and it will save millions of rupees in multistoried building annually.

Rain Collecting Skyscraper

A lot of plants especially plamaceae family is a good source of inspiration to build skyscrapers for harvesting rain water. By simply observing plants like coconut, araecnut, bottle palm and many other palmate compound leaves during the rainy season you can visualize that these plants collect the rain water very interestingly and pour the water directly at the base of the plant through the un-branched trunk. Why can't we apply this secret in our skyscrapers and other miniature building so that we can collect the wash out rain water and millions of gallon rain water waste every year? Here comes the two young researchers from Polish Ryszard

Rychlicki and Agnieszka Nowak constructed H3AR received recognition recently and awarded a prestigious recognition in Poland.

Artificial Solar Cell

The secret of producing energy by green plants when hitting sunlight inspired many to develop "green energy". Professor Nathan Nelson of Tel Aviv University discovered a complex membrane protein which can produce green energy at its center. center. He extracted PSI(Photosystem1) super complex crystal from pea plant and suggested it may be used as small battery which charges when it illuminated. It am y also be used as a core of solar cell. It is also observed that when this PSI is packed in crystals, then it can be use to electricity from light energy in an electronic device. An amazing observation is that hen this system is packed in gold covered plat; we are able to generate about 10 volt. Professor Farrant's observation of seed dormancy and its mechanism by tolerating extreme environmental condition and its resurrection on re-watering is path finder for more sophisticated study on this line. The secret of resurrection will assists us to live healthy and happily in extreme climate condition that happened in many part of the world during summer and cold seasons. This may help us to survives instead of thousands of death occurring yearly due to extreme heat and cold.

Artificial Photosynthesis

Photosynthesis is one of the common words in mind of any school gone children from lower Kg to

PG. But, the question in front of biomimcry is that, can we reproduce this world's largest anabolic reaction by our won will, then it might be the noblest Nobel prize winning discovery in the future. The process could make hydrogen fuel cells an efficient, self-recharging and less expensive way to create and store energy applicable in home and industrial systems. If this process could be reproduced artificially, it will create a world without poverty and equality will be the result.

Innovative idea from Tape root system

A taproot is, as its name implies, a main root that burrows almost vertically down into the soil to stabilize the tree in high winds. Because it is a continuation of the trunk downward into the soil, the stiff taproot essentially resists lateral forces applied to the above-ground tree by "pushing back" against the soil in the opposite direction. Further stability is provided by ramifying lateral roots that extend outward near the soil surface (Vogel1996). Stiffness, or resistance to bend, along with sufficient breadth, or "broad-side" area, are critical features in taproots: too much flexion decreases above-ground stability, while a too-narrow root may penetrate sideways through the soil rather than "pushing" against it(Vogel 1996). The limber pine is one example of an organism that has put the taproot to good use. The pine thrives in windswept areas due in large part to the anchoring of its tough, thick taproot. Further study of the taproot's structure, composition, and trunk-root relationship may lead to innovations in building foundations, columns, piles and caissons, and other structural support elements.

Inspiration from jack pine

The jack pine is often heralded as the most fire-adapted of all boreal conifers. One of the main reasons for this is its reproductive strategy. Although the tree itself may die in a fire, its seeds usually survive. In fact, the fire is necessary for the release and dispersal of the jack pine's resin-sealed, cone-encased seeds. As a jack pine cone heats up above 60 degrees Celsius, the resin melts, and seeds are scattered onto the forest floor. The seeds remain viable provided that the wings do not ignite and the outer coating does not crack. Such damage happens only with prolonged heat exposure and/or temperatures above 400 degrees Celsius, neither of which are common in crown fires. Serotiny provides a model for that might inspire innovation in several different aspects of fire protection. A serotiny-inspired system could serve as a smoke—or heat-detector, with components changing their phase or spatial position when exposed to the stimulus. Serotinous cones are also an example of how fire can be utilized, rather than redirected, resisted, or extinguished.

The liverwort

The liverwort is a small, green nonvascular plant that grows in wet places and resembles nothing so much as green seaweed or leafy moss. It uses an abiotic seed dispersal mechanism called splash-cup, which takes advantage of the hydraulic pressure of falling water to disperse seeds. The cup works this way: rainwater dripping off foliage above, drips into the splash cup.

The cup is just the right shape and size so that when the water hits the bottom of the cup, it splashes out with enough force to disperse the (seeds/spores) up to a meter away (Brodie, 1975). What makes the liverwort's dispersal mechanism so interesting is that it is a structural arrangement that takes advantage of an already extant external source of energy. Thus, the plant itself need not devote its own energy to seed dispersal. The liverwort might inspire innovation in materials distribution and exchange-systems.

The maple tree

The maple tree has developed strategies that enable it to withstand, and even work with, high winds. The broad, toothy, three-lobed structure of the maple leaf is the result of several selective pressures. First, the leaf must fulfill its principal function of gathering sunlight, and a broad, flat surface area is best for this purpose. But the broad surface area is also well-suited to capturing radiant heat, thus increasing the likelihood that the leaf may overheat while gathering sunlight. One of the most efficient cooling methods is convection, or the transfer of excess heat to air moving across a surface. The jagged margins of the maple leaf enhance convection by preventing air from piling up in stagnant boundary layers. And finally, the lobed architecture of the maple leaf is an elegant and simple solution to wind drag. A broad, flat leaf behaves in much the same way as a flag would in a wind, flapping and snapping, subject to drag and the resultant wear-and-tear. But when a gust of air hits the lobed maple leaf, it rolls its side lobes inward, creating a cone through which wind easily passes. The stronger is the wind, the tighter the cone. The maple has one other strategy that takes advantage of the wind; it uses wind to disperse its seeds. Commonly called 'whirly-birds' or 'helicopters', maple seeds are equipped with a single, membranous wing that provides lift in a breeze, and a spinning descent in still air. The wing of a maple seed is pitched slightly, much like a propeller blade. What makes the maple leaf adaptations so interesting is that they offer simple, elegant structural solutions to several different problems: how to maximize energy-capture while minimizing the negative effects of heat absorption and wind resistance. The maple leaf strategies—lobed architecture and jagged margins—may offer insights into how one might design buildings, automobiles, airplanes, and even clothing to withstand and respond to changing wind conditions.

Inspiration from Okra

A native of North Africa, okra is a tall (3-6 feet), annual vegetable, now grown worldwide for its sticky, ribbed green pods. Okra, along with a few other species of the abelmoschus genus (moschatus and tetraphyllus) alters the permeability of its seed coat in response to ambient humidity levels. The seed coat of okra contracts and the palisade cell layer thickens when exposed to dry conditions. Palisade cells are closely packed, columnar cells, lying in the upper region of seeds. When these cells thicken along with the seed coat contraction, the surface of the seed becomes harder and impermeable, conserving valuable water within the seed (Villavicencio, 2002). The okra's strategy might inspire innovation in building envelope and apparel design.

Inspiration from Artemisia plant

The Artemisia plant, *Artemesia iwayomogi*, a native of Korea, produces an essential oil containing antibacterial agents that inhibits the growth of bacteria. Essential oils are scented or bioactive chemicals called terpenoids (similar to alkaloids, phenols, etc.) that possess a chemical aromatic structure. Various components of essential oils exhibit antibacterial activity: camphor, 1,8-cineole, borneol, camphene, and beta-caryophyllene. The Artemisia plant produces an oil that exhibits antibacterial activity against six Gram-positive and six Gram-negative bacteria. The antibacterial properties of the oil may be attributed to the terpenoids, camphor, 1,8-cineole, borneol, camphene, and beta-caryophyllene (**Yu, 2003**). The essential oil of the Artemisia plant might inspire innovation in the detergents/soaps industry (antibacterial cleaners), the kitchen/bath counter industry (antibacterial surfaces), and interior designs (scents connected to antibacterial properties).

Inspiration from Eucalyptus trees

Eucalyptus trees flourish in fire-scorched country thanks to several key adaptations. Those eucalypt species known as 'candlebarks' have bark that acts as a sacrificial shield. Hanging from the trunk in long, flammable strips, the bark ignites when exposed to flame, and then falls away from the tree, saving the cambium from conflagration. The presence of epicormic buds just beneath the bark of the trunk and stem indicate yet another fire adaptive strategy. They lurk, dormant, just beneath the bark surface, held in check by growth substances produced by the leaves and shoots above. When leaves and shoots are destroyed by fire, the check is removed, and the buds are allowed to sprout. The green foliage that cloaks eucalyptus trunks after a fire is the product of epicormic buds. Often, such foliage is the tree's only source of photosynthetic activity following a fire, and so is crucial for its survival. A final fire adaptation among eucalypts is the lignotuber. Lignotubers are root swellings, located at the base of the tree or beneath the soil surface, in which food and shoot-forming structures are stored. After a fire, lignotubers not only generate new shoots, but feed them until normal photosynthetic levels and processes resume. What makes the eucalypt family of trees so interesting is that they employ several diverse strategies to both resist and use fire. The diversification of strategies and mechanisms allows them to thrive in areas and under circumstances that may prove detrimental to other species. The eucalyptus might inspire innovation in fire detection, suppression, and utilization, enabling engineers to develop adaptive response systems that employ a wide range of tactics, each designed to be implemented at different fire stages.

Inspiration form Florida rosemary

The Florida rosemary is a characteristic evergreen shrub of the Florida scrub. It is well-adapted for drought, wind, and periodic wildfire. The small surface area of its needle-like leaves limits water loss through evaporation. The overall round shape of the shrub confers protection against buffeting winds. And its toxic chemical secretions prevent the growth of underlying vegetation, reducing not only competition but also potential fuel sources. This strategy, called allelopathy, helps to maintain the scrub community at large, since most scrub species regenerate best when exposed to crown fires every 20-60 years. But the Florida rosemary's strategies are not limited to fire resistance: when fire finally does occur, the parent rosemary dies, but its seeds, buried in the soil and until now inhibited through allelopathy, rapidly germinate, and begin the cycle anew. The Florida rosemary's numerous survival strategies are instructive on several levels. It has developed mechanisms for water retention, wind resistance, fire utilization and resistance, and competitor control. The rosemary might inspire innovation in building envelope design, apparel design, water distribution and storage, and fire-protection systems.

Inspiration from giant sequoia

Among fire-adapted tree species, there are resisters and embracers. Resisters are those species that avoid fire damage through use of insulating bark, self-pruning, and specialized shape. The goal of the resister is to survive a fire. Embracers, by contrast, depend upon fire for the survival of the species, if not of the individual tree. Embracers may rely on fire to open seed cases or cones, and to condition the soil for germination. The giant sequoia is unusual in that it is simultaneously a resister and an embrace. Its bark is two to four feet thick, effectively insulating the underlying cambium from the heat of a fire. Its canopy is elevated and its lower branches self-prune, reducing the likelihood of torching.

Its sap is based on water rather than resin, and acts as a fire retardant for the tree. At the same time, it exhibits the embracer trait of serotiny, or delayed seed release. The cones of the giant sequoia must be desiccated or mechanically scarred in order to release their seeds; after a fire, a single tree can scatter millions of seeds. The seeds take root in the bare mineral soil exposed by the fire, and are nourished by sunlight that enters through openings in the canopy created by fire. The adaptations of the giant sequoia are instructive in several ways. Rather than relying on only one strategy to deal with fire, it has evolved several mechanisms that work in concert to prolong not only the life of the individual tree, but also to improve the likelihood of reproductive success and thus survival of the species. What makes the sequoia interesting is that it approaches the "problem" of fire from two perspectives: resistance and dependence. In essence, for the giant sequoia, fire is not a threat or detriment, but an essential component to survival. The giant sequoia's strategies might inspire innovation in fire protection systems, materials, and mechanisms, particularly at the building scale.

Inspiration from Guayule plant

When tapped for rubber, the guayule shrub excretes a resinous byproduct. The resin repels and/or kills termites, as well as repelling brown-rot, white-rot, and other fungi. The resin's anti-termitic and anti-fungal properties are attributable to the presence of several eudesmane-type sesquiterpenoids. What makes guayule resin interesting is that the plant appears to provide an alternative and renewable source of wood preservatives.

The resin might inspire innovation in such industries as wood preservation, construction, building materials, and bath and tile. "Impregnation of guayule resin extract into wood at 50% and higher is needed to make the wood resistant to termite attack. At the highest level of 97% resin content, complete termite mortality was achieved" (Nakayama, 2001). "The guayule resin extract when impregnated into the southern pine made it resistant to fungal attack. Resistance to *G. traveum* started at 10.3% resin content and 51.8% for P. placenta. At resin contents of 51.8% and higher, the treated wood was highly resistant (*G. traveum*). In a similar manner, the specific gravity change was less at the higher resin contents. Bultman *et al.* (1991) reported that the resin material inhibited the activity of several types of brown-rot (*Gleophyllum trabeum, Antrodia carbonica, Fomitopsis cajanderi, and Lentinus Ponderosa*) and white-rot (*Dichomitus squalens, Trametes versiclor, and Ganodermas sp.*) fungi. Maatooq *et al.*, (1996) identified several eudesmane-type sesquiterpenoids extracted from the guayule plant that had antifungal activities" (Nakayama, 2000). The roots of the red mangrove tree, like those of most members of the Mangroaceae family, use a unique two-part system to anchor the tree firmly in the loose soil of marshes and bays.

Inspiration from Red mangrove

Early in its life, the red mangrove grows aerial, or prop, roots, so named because a good portion of the root is above the surface of the water, arching outward to support the tree. An arch is one of the strongest architectural configurations and indeed, prop roots are so sturdy that, although they usually measure less than an inch in diameter, one can walk along them without causing them to break. As the tree matures, it also grows drop roots, which descend from the branches and provide the second anchoring component. In a flood, mangrove roots function not only to hold the tree in place, but to filter out sediment and debris washed from inland areas that would otherwise flow into the ocean. If left unfiltered, inland runoff can make ocean water cloudy, blocking the sunlight required by coral and sea grass. What makes the red mangrove's anchoring strategies so interesting is that they are simple, structural solutions to the problem of stability and endurance in flood prone areas. It is also instructive to note that the plant has built in redundancies (two anchoring systems) and that these anchors perform indirect and wholly unrelated functions (sediment and debris capture). The prop and drop roots of the red mangrove might inspire innovation in building design in flood prone areas, as well as the material sciences. They may also inspire innovations in systems design, in which a single component or structure may serve several unrelated functions.

Inspiration from Seed coat

The hilar valve of the hard seeds of some desert plants responds to changes in humidity levels in the environment, controlling the seed coat's permeability to moisture. The hilar valve responds to ambient relative humidity (RH). During periods of high RH (70% or above), the valve opens to allow water exchange between the seed's interior and the external environment. During periods of low RH, the valve closes, making the seed coat impermeable, thereby keeping interior water content at a steady state.

However, the seed coat's impermeability is strictly one-way: water vapor is able to enter the seed during all conditions, but water loss is strictly regulated by the valve. This adaptation is critical for the survival of desert plants. What makes the hilar valve interesting is that it can sense and then respond appropriately to subtle changes in humidity in the environment. Even more surprising is its ability to control the unequal exchange of water across the seed coating: it can prohibit or limit water loss while not inhibiting water intake. The hilar valve's unique approach to regulating water exchange might inspire innovation in building designs and the apparel industry.

Inspiration from Strangler-fig

Hemiepiphytic figs are able to survive fire due to a combination of shape and rejuvenation strategies. Their spatial configuration is such that foliage is located high in the canopy of the host tree, out of the reach of flames. Their aerial roots are vulnerable to conflagration, but these can be sacrificed, with new roots sent down after the fire has passed. The fire-resistant strategies of the strangler fig are interesting because they rely on a host-parasite relationship. Its ability to withstand fire as a result of location relies solely on its tendency to grow high in the branches of other trees. Its ability to survive the loss of aerial roots is due to a built-in redundancy: when it's supply lines (roots) are destroyed in a fire, it can rely temporarily on nutrients taken from its host tree. While it isn't clear what advantages the host tree may gain from the relationship, it is obvious that the advantages of location and alternative energy supply conferred upon the parasitic fig are central to its ability to withstand fire. The fig might inspire innovation in building design and fire-protection systems.

Inspiration from Taquari bamboo

Whereas most bamboo plants make their home in wet or humid habitats, the taquari can be found in the cerrado, or dry scrubland, of central Brazil. It has several important adaptations to protect it from dessication and fire damage. The buds of the culm, or main stem, are covered with hard scales that prevent water loss. The thick walls and pithy interior of the culm work both to retain water and insulate the plant against fire. (The solid nature of the taquari culm is another feature that sets it apart from its kin; most bamboos are hollow). At the base of the culm, either at ground level or just beneath, are specialized buds that remain dormant until the culm has been scorched. Triggered by fire, the buds break their dormancy and produce clusters of shoots. These shoots take on the appearance and function of the killed culms, growing tall and erect, and re-branching from buds on the lower nodes. What makes the taquari interesting is that it employs three strategies to protect itself against fire damage and dessication. It uses shielding in the form of soil, bud scales, and thick culm walls to insulate growth tissues against heat. It uses rejuvenation to regrow culms killed by fire. And it adjusts its shape so that these rejuvenating structures are located at or beneath the soil surface, where they are

Ashokan Kannarath

less likely to burn. The taquari might inspire innovation in fire protection systems that rely on modifications in materials, structural design, and location. It might also inspire innovation in systems aimed at using rather than fighting fire.

Inspiration from Tarbush

The tarbush produces volatile chemicals suspended in essential oils that protect the tarbush from fungi, termites, and predation by herbivores. The primary components are sesquiterpenoids, such as beta-caryophyllene, alpha-humulene, germacrene D; and, monoterpenoids, such as myrcene, 3-omega-carene, limonene, and omega-selinene. The hexane fraction of the essential oil exhibits anti-fungal activity; as little as 1 mg is sufficient to deter fungal activity in bioautography assays (Tellez, 2001). Termites are successfully deterred by the diethyl ether fraction of the essential oil (Tellez, 2001). "The essential oil of the hexanes extract was consistently more active against fungi than the extract itself, suggesting that a good portion of the activity in the hexanes extract resides in its steam-distilled volatile components. Several major volatile components, pinene (2.0%), 3-carene (12.6%), limonene (27.7%) (Himejima *et al.*, 1992), and eudesmol (11.3%) (Miyakado etal, 1976) are reported to have antifungal activity. Another major component, myrcene (19.9%), is reported to enhance the activity of other antimicrobials" (Tellez, 2001). One way that the tarbush chemicals deter grazing by sheep and other herbivores is by disrupting digestive microbes in their gastrointestinal tracts. What makes tarbush leaf compounds interesting is that they are made with local materials and simple ingredients found within the organism, created at organism temperature, and produced on an as-needed basis. The compounds are also biodegradable. The tarbush might inspire innovation in paint manufacturers (protective coatings and finishes), the construction industry (prolong material life through rot/mold resistance), wood preservation (anti-rot, anti-mold, termite resistance), and the bath and tile industry (anti-mildew surfaces, grout).

Inspiration from Tea plant

The tea family, Theaceae, includes evergreen trees and shrubs found in temperate and tropical regions of both hemispheres. One such shrub, found at the rainy summit of Cerro de la Neblina in southern Venezuela, is noteworthy for its fire resistance. In a stand ignited by lightning, Neblinaria celiae had a 93 percent survival rate, compared to zero survival of seven co-occurring woody species. Neblinaria's ability to withstand fire can be attributed to two mechanisms: shielding and shape. Its thick bark and massive rosettes, or leaf clusters, insulate the plant's growth tissues. Its sparse branching pattern and maximized upward growth keep foliage well off the ground, reducing their exposure to fire. The Neblinaria's fire-protection strategy is interesting because it relies on both material and structural elements to provide protection and increase the chance of survival. In addition, these strategies do not appear to hinder the plant's competitiveness in times between fires. Then too, the strategies do not require the production and use of toxic synthetic materials, but instead rely upon a specific arrangement of materials produced naturally. The

Neblinaria might inspire innovations in fire protection systems, particularly those based on structural and material modifications.

Inspiration from White-rot fungi

This fungus has a property in that when the spores are inoculated into soil, it increases water repellency without affecting soil porosity. It also removing microorganisms from soil—produce extra cellular polysaccharide sheaths (White, 2000)—degrade hard cell walls of microorganisms using peroxidase and oxidase systems (see quote)—"white-rot group of basidiomycete fungi is capable of degrading ligno-cellulosic material via extracellular, non-specific, free radical generating peroxidase and oxidase systems. Thus, they are uniquely able to non-specifically decay a broad spectrum of structurally diverse organic compounds, including many aromatic xenobiotics" (White, 2000). What makes white-rot fungi interesting is that they are a naturally occurring biodegrading agent that is easily added to soils. In addition, their presence increases water repellency which stabilizes and strengthens soil. The fungi use local, simple, nontoxic, biodegradable chemicals. White-rot fungi might inspire innovation in construction (cementation of soil), building materials (remove water-loving elements of materials that cause rot), and in strengthening soil-to-structure anchoring in building foundations.

Vaccine preservation solution from
Myrothamnus *flabellifolia*

This plant is unique due to its property of resurrect itself. It is originate d and native plant of South Africa. It is very popular there because of its wide spread medical use, traditionally. Then chemical produce by this plant cells can be used to produce vaccine, which cannot need cold storage and hence can be transported distant place without losing its property. This vaccine are vaporized with coating of athelarosa, hence it become inert substance. In this inert condition it can be packed and kept in cabinet in store house. It also can be transported for long distance without causing any degradation. In the store house it can be stored for month.

CHAPTER-4

Inspiration derived from Animal kingdom

Mimicking Sea Cucumbers: Medical Solutions

When you look at a sea cucumber—an ocean floor-dwelling animal that looks like a giant slug—medical solutions might not be the first item that pops into your mind. A sea cucumber's skin is soft and flexible to help it navigate obstacles as it travels along the ocean floor. When a threat arises, our unlikely hero's skin quickly transforms into a hard, rigid protective shield. As soon as the threat dissipates, the sea cucumber again relaxes and goes along on its way. Christoph Weder and Stuart Rowan, researchers and professors at Case Western Reserve University, have created a new material that mimics the sea cucumber's ability to transition between states of rigidity. Their bio-inspired material has resulted in a surprising new medical application. Currently, paralyzed patients can get an electronic device—called a neural electrode—implanted into their brain to help send and receive brain messages. The electrodes are typically made of metal, ceramic or silicon, but such brittle materials can cause brain tissue damage over prolonged periods of time. On top of this sobering fact, the cells in the brain—in response to the foreign object—will attack the electrode, significantly decreasing the electrode's recording ability and eventually causing it to fail. Weder and Rowan's material is being applied to neural electrodes that are rigid enough to insert in the brain, but once they come into contact with the brain's water, they will become soft and flexible enough to avoid the brain tissue damage that current electrodes cause.

This species of sea cucumber is called the Holothuria Argus and believe it or not, this sea cucumber is humongous! If you were to pick it up, it would be as long as your arms . . . stretched out

The material that these scientists created to mimic the sea cucumber's ability is, according to Weder, "Cool because it can rapidly shift between a dynamic range of flexibility and rigidity." Within the skin of the sea cucumber, the rigid nano-rods are made from collagen, a protein. The rods do not interact with each other when the sea cucumber is relaxed, but when the organism feels threatened it releases a protein that binds to the collagen, and cross links all the rigid rods, essentially creating a scaffold that stiffens the skin. The basic mechanism that Rowan and Weder are mimicking is control over the interaction of the rods. Their material also mimics the matrix architecture of the sea cucumber's skin. Weder noted, "Once you understand the architecture, the basic process, we can say, well, we can do this with a different material, with different chemistry, and different ingredients certainly not as sophisticated as nature does it, but we can make materials that can change their properties." Instead of using collagen, which is in sea cucumber skin, Rowan and Weder used cellulose—an easy-to-use and accessible protein—from tunicates (an underwater filter feeding organism). They used the cellulose from tunicates because their fibers are especially long and thus the researchers could use a relatively small amount for testing. The scientists noted that once the material is manufactured, however, cellulose could be taken from wood, cotton, or wheat, all of which are renewable, easily accessible resources that could even be taken from recycled waste products. Rowan and Weder embedded the cellulose fibers into a pliable plastic, which yielded a rigid material. The hydroxyl groups (molecules consisting of oxygen and hydrogen) on the surface of the cellulose fibers stick together, forming a fibrous web. To break the fiber bonds and loosen the web, Weder and Rowan's team injected a water-based solvent, which was an artificial cerebral spinal fluid used to mimic the fluid in the brain. The hydrogen groups of the solvent bond with those on the cellulose fibers, and as a result the fibers decouple from one another. Conversely, as the water evaporates, the cellulose fibers reconnect and the material becomes stiff again. The researchers used water as the "switch" because of their desire to insert neural electrodes made of the material into the human brain, but they also would like to come up with other ways to switch the material, such as electrically, chemically, with light.

Discovering Success:

In terms of the success of their project, Weder said, "As scientists we are delighted that we could take nature's architecture and we could mimic the function in a very crude way. That in and of itself is a success." They recently published an article in Science magazine about their research on the bio-inspired material. Despite this scientific victory, "There's a lot more to it before we can make a product," stated Rowan. He continued, "All we've done is prove concept, and now we are working on the product. We are trying to understand the process in a lot more detail, and how to control it." The Advanced Platform Technology Veteran's Affairs Medical Center and the National Institute of Health (NIH) approached Weder and Rowan to apply their new material to the neural electrode. Testing is currently underway to ensure the efficacy of the electrodes. There is a plethora of potential applications for this material. The National Science Foundation (NSF) recently began funding Weder and Rowan to apply the material to electrically switchable medical braces, also called orthotic devices or "smart" casts. The braces would be stiff to support broken body parts, but when the patient needed surgery or to rotate within the brace, it could become flexible with the push of a button.

Looking to Nature

Since their research on the sea cucumber, the scientists have begun to look to nature for further inspiration. Weder stated, "I'm sure that I could learn a lot from nature by going out and asking, 'What other cool animals are out there? What other cool tricks are out there that have not been researched to death?'" Rowan added that, "There are a lot of animals that do incredibly cool things that at the moment we cannot do. A lot of this is cutting edge stuff, just figuring out how organisms do what they do." Rowan and Weder have ideas about future research involving biomimicry (imitating nature's designs and processes to solve human problems) and have "other inspirations" from nature, but they claim that it is too early to talk about them. Despite all the unknowns of the future, Rowan stated, "I think this whole process has changed how I look at science, to the point that I look more at what nature does. I look at nature a different way as well because of this process."

Shinkansen Bullet Train: Inspired by Kingfisher

Bulletin train is traveling at speed of 187 mph (300km/h, a breakneck speed, amazing. Every man made things has one or more demerit, here also the case is not different. *Shinkansen Bullet Train* definitely has an alarming speed but it cause an equally alarming sound, people cloud not bear the exploding sound of the train. Thed complaint about unbearable sound to human being piled up day by day. The unending request, from locals and other segment of employees related with railway, to abandon or reduce the drum breaking sound is daily occurrence. Authorities of railway forced to think about the ban of these train. The train is harsher when it reach tunnels, here the sound zoom beyond mega decibel. Biomimcry give an idea, how to reduce the mega decibel of this train. Engineer and biomimcry scientists' thing about it and finally nature came to the rescue in the form of a minute creature, a bird, Kingfisher. It is a common observation that kingfisher swooped into water to catch its prey in an breakneck speed, that also without producing and sort of sound and even no buzzzz. Engineers thought, if we can copy the secret and apply the same principle in the case of bulletin train, we can avoid the drum breaking sound of the train soon. The secret of the kingfisher lies in its beak; it is so constructed that it partitions the air in such a speed that it cannot make even a flash and so no sound. This secret is now apply in al sort of train that has amazing speed like bullet train When the engineers construct such a design the train with 10% more speed and 15 % less energy. Thanks to the beautiful kingfisher. The creature of Mother Nature, we salute to you.

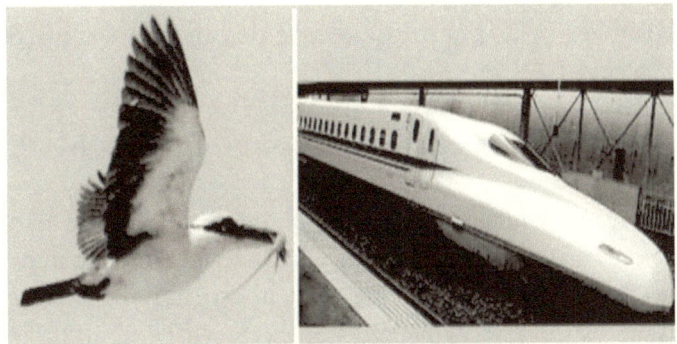

Kingfisher Shinkansen Bullet Train
(Source: Wikimedia Commons)
(Source: Filmage Public Domain)

Speedo Fastskin: Inspired by Shark skin i

The shark skin, a leathery, thick spiny, rough outer covering of the shark inspired biomimcry engineers in fascinating way. The skin of shark is embedded with many tiny scales called placoid scale. It is trident scale with three spiny points projecting on the surface and gives it rough appearance. The shark use this scales in different forms of arrangement to navigate through sea water with different rate flow of water at different depth and conditions. The arrangement of scales in different decoration design will increase the speed of the shark in any kind of waves and even in the whirlpool. If this secret we copy and make a suit, it will help the deep divers or swimmers to navigate the harsh environment in the surface and deeper part of the sea. Engineers finally constructed such a suit, now called Fastskin. Another product based on the inspiration derived from shark skin is Speedo, a swimwear. The company Speedo now emerged as multimillion turnover one. The most recent design of Fastskin is Fsatskin FZR racer.

Anti-reflective coating: Inspiration from Moth

It is common knowledge that any surface can reflect a part of light falling on it, even a transparent glass surface. In the case of nocturnal organisms like moth, the reflection of even a bit of light is dangerous as it will become a prey for the predators, but at the same time it must need light to navigate in the darkness. The creator of the nature given such a fantastic structure eye that can do both of these in an amazing manner. The eye of moth is provided with very little but multiple protrusions. These protrusions will minimize reflection and at the same time increase the light absorption. This moth protects themselves from predators and getting sufficient light to get over darkness of the night. Now days this principle is copied in the preparation of eye glass or sunglasses with anti-reflector film coating. The product based on this principle not ending in sunglass but, see the screen of mobile phone, computer screens, photography lenses, telescopes etc also based on the same principle.

In the case of sunglass it give relief to human eye, but in the case of photography lenses it increase the clarity of the photo or videos.

Fiber Optic Design inspired from Sponges (Porifera)

A species of marine sponge known as *Rossella racovitzae*, is an inspiration to biomimcry engineers recently. As all the sponges it also has Spicule, the endo-skeleton of the proferans. This sponge living in the depth of sea where light is negligible, but the Spicule is able to collect light sufficient to do photosynthesis to subsist the creature in the dark, deep sea. The light actually need for the green coloured single celled algae living in the sponge for photosynthesis. Today the light capturing property of this Spicule is the inspiration for the designing of fiber optics. Optical fibers transmit large amount of information encoded as a light pulses through a long distance. It is also interesting to note that, if laser beams are transmitting through fiber optics the communication speed become much faster than the traditional one. You know, a fiber strand not less than a hair thick contain about 100 optical fibers and it can transmit about 40,000 different sound channels. Today fiber optic also used to reflect light to skyscraper where direct light is not accessible. Huge lenses are fitted at the top of the skyscrapers which reflect light to the end of fiber optic transmitter, which then send light to the required spot in the buildings. The sponge also do the same thing, it capture light in a very efficient manner by its fiber optic like Spicule and reflects it the surroundings where light not at all reach. This beneficial not only to the sponge itself but also to other organism dwelling in the deepest part of the Antarctica ocean(10-200 meter depth) where light cannot reach and remain in total darkness. You may wonder by knowing the fact that, the sponge prepares this fiber optics at low temperature with low coast materials and without spending huge amount and sophisticated machinery.

Aerodynamics: Inspired from Fruit flies

Fruit fly is ideal source for copying aerodynamic secretes. It uses more than one aerodynamic feature. When they fly it leaves a whirlpool of air current behind, it is more severe than the whirlpool created by a wake of ship. The flight muscle of fruit fly is also very efficient as it cause 200 times flap of wing (2.5mm) per second, it is not seen any other insect. The same type flight in aerodynamic machine causes different complexities like breaking of wings, heat generation and burning etc. But the insect solve all these problems by a series of hooks called hamuli. The hamuli join the front and hind wings together while flying. When the flies land the hooks separate and fold up against the body. Along with the hook mechanism other features like sharp eye elytra flapping to balance and other minute structures make the flight more successful in insects.

Pit viper: Inspiration for Missile detection

The pit viper or *Crotalines* is an interesting animal for biomimcry engineers recently. The pit organ of this snake is more interested one; it is a small nerve-rich pit in front of the eye of the snake. The snake uses this pit to locate the homoeothermic (Warm blooded) animals in its vicinity. The pit contains very advanced heat sensitive machinery which can sense a rat several meters away in the darkness. The snakes ability to search and destroy the prey is very fascinating one that we can use the same system to detect the missile of enemy country and destruct it. It also can be used in flight by pilots to detect unknown enemy attacks, especially by air force troops. But still the engineers are not able to mimic the pit organs as such with same precision as pit viper employing; finally we are copying and creators as God. To study the details of the vipers activity we can use living on site photography and serial video shootings, still the mechanism is so complicate that we cannot measure the impulse end the nerve during the activity. But let us hope that the secret will explore very soon.

Chameleon as a camouflage model

The ability of changing colour by chameleon is always fascinated to human. This changing colour is within a short period of time is more amazing one. This change in colour is with the help of special cell called chromatophore. The chromatophore contains basic pigments yellow and red. The reflective layer by the same time reflects the blue and white light rays. To darken the color the melanophore contains black to dark brown pigments. Chameleon not only changes the color as per the surrounding single colour but also make variety of shade to match exactly the surroundings. The actual secret lies in this spontaneous colur change are due to the contraction and expansion of the skin. This principle can be transferred to prepare cloths, bags, hats and shoes etc. The fiber specially developed to change color with battery fitted are using today for changing colour of the cloth, but is very expensive (around 10,000 USD). We hope that engineers will success in preparing cloth which change color as we go to party where, when the color lit our cloth also will change color as the surroundings.

The beetle Stenocara:
A new method for water collection

Animals in desert are very rare and those present shows extreme adaptations of various kind. Some organism shows astonishing designs. Tenebrinoid is one such organism, the beetle *Stenocara,* which lives in the Namib Desert, in Southern Africa. The water capture system by these insect is very amazing. The beetle has tiny bumps on its back. The region between the bumps is free of waxy coating. This wax free region collects water vapor from atmosphere, even in small quantity. The problem is, when the water collect on the bumps it will evaporate immediately as heat and wind is frequent occurrence in desert. In that situation the beetle tilt its body along the ground and the droplet formed is rolled on the wing is slipped into its mouth. The tiny bumps help to produce the droplets. If this bumpy structure we imitate in building roofs, water trapping tent or water condensers and engines, water can be collected very easily. This amazing creation is one of the examples that nature's creation is errorless.

Locust Method for Traffic Problems

Thousands of death is occurring due to road accident daily in all parts of the world. Locust, an insect can provide us a solution for the traffic problems. Locusts swarms in millions and move fast without colliding with each other. It is experimentally proved that locust send electronic signals which can identify by other locust so avoid the way and collision. If the same technique can imitate by adapting some device which produce electronic signals and can detect by another vehicle collision can be avoided. But it needs sophisticated study and experiment. We hope that it will become practicable in the near future.

Self-Changing Display Signs: Inspired by Peacock Feathers

The colour impact in peacock is due to the refraction of keratin protein and melanin pigment, the only pigment present in the peacock feather. The directional layering of the keratin produces the light and dark colour of the feather. Peacock feathers' exceedingly bright hues stem from this structural feature. Nature inspired one Japanese company to develop reusable display signs, whose surfaces are structurally altered under ultraviolet light which changes the material's crystalline alignment, thus eliminating certain colors so as to display the desired message. These signs can be used over and over and imprinted with new images. This eliminates the cost of producing new signs, as well as the need for using toxic paints

Butterfly: A Computer Solution

Computer is the parts and parcel of life today. Without computer the life become impossible now days. We use computer in office, house, shops, schools, colleges, universities etc. one of the quality determining factors in computer is its speed. The speed of the computer is in turn depends upon the chips used in it. When we use better chips it cost more electricity consumption, because the advanced chips will heat up easily. So to reduce the heat and their by reduce the electricity bill is essentially necessary. How can we do this? Butterfly will give us an idea in this line. The wings of the butter fly are studded with many tiny scales. These scales form thin films. This film dissipates the heat generated during its flapping. So to improve the speed of the computer we can incorporate better chips with cooling system like butterfly scales. Then we can reduce the heating of the chips and electricity consumption.

From the Immune System, a Solution to the Computer Virus Menace

Once a single computer is affected by a virus, this means that other computers in the world may soon be contaminated as well. Many companies, therefore, have seen it necessary to set up an "immune system" to protect their network systems from viruses and continue to carry out intensive research in this area. One of the centers that is carrying out this work is the virus isolation laboratory at the IBM's Watson Research Center in New York. There, a high-security microbiology laboratory works with lethal viruses, also producing programs that can diagnose the 12,000 or so viruses identified so far—and also isolate the viruses from a computer in a safe manner and then kill them. IBM is only one of the firms trying to construct a worldwide immune system to protect its existing computer systems from virus threats in the cyberspace. Steve White, one of the company's executives, states that to achieve that end, an immune system like the human bodies is needed. It's only the existence of an immune system that allows the human race to exist. Only an immune system in cyberspace will allow it to exist (Kurt Kleiner, 1997). Pursuing this analogy between the computer and living things, researchers have begun producing protective programs that function like our own immune systems. They believe what we have learnt from epidemiology (the branch of science which studies contagious diseases) and immunology (which deals with the immune system) will be able to protect electronic programs from new threats in the same way that antibodies protect living organisms.

Computer viruses are clever self-replicating programs designed to infiltrate computers, multiply by copying themselves and damage or "hijack" the computers they enter. Indications that such viruses are present include a slowing down of the computer system, occasional mysterious damage to files, and sometimes, complete failure or "crashing" of the computer itself—much as with the various diseases that affects human beings. To protect our computers against the menace of viruses, identification programs search every code in the computer's memory to find traces of viruses that have previously been identified and stored in the programs' memory. Computer viruses carry traces of the signature of the software writer that let them be recognized. When the computer's search program recognizes that telltale signature, it warns that the computer has been infected with a virus. Even so, anti-virus programs can't offer complete protection for computers. Some programmers can write new viruses within a matter of a few days and again insert them into cyberspace through just one infected computer. That being the case, it's vital that anti-virus programs be constantly updated so that they have the information they need to recognize new viruses. New anti-virus programs need to be added constantly, therefore, to protect against the virus threat.

With the increasing spread of worldwide use of the Internet, these viruses have begun to spread very much faster and to inflict serious harm to infected computers. IBM researchers have found solutions by imitating natural examples. First of all, just like biological viruses in nature, artificial computer viruses use the host programming to multiply. Starting from that analogy, researchers investigated how the human immune system works to protect the body. When it encounters a foreign organism, the body immediately begins to build antibodies that will recognize the invader and destroy it. The immune system doesn't need to analyze the whole of a cell that might result in a sickness. Once any preliminary infection has been suppressed, the body keeps a number of the appropriate antibodies in readiness, to respond immediately to any future recurrence. Thanks to these standby antibodies, there is no need to examine the entire infected cell. Similarly, existing anti-virus programs also contain an "antibody" that recognizes not the whole computer virus, but rather its signature. As we have seen, the solutions to many problems in the technical arena that leave us floundering already exist in nature. Our immune system, of which every detail has been thought out and which functions perfectly, was ready to protect us before we were even born.

Eye to the Camera: the Technology of Sight

Light enters the eye through pupil, a spherical opening in the eye of vertebrates. Lens located behind the pupil. Light fires enter the eye through the pupil, then pass through the lens and enter into a fluid called humor and last strike the retina, a photosensitive layer in the eye. In the retina there are about 100 million light sensitive cells known as rods and cones. The rod cells are for light and dark vision, and the cones detect colors. All these cells turn the light falling onto them into electrical impulse and send them to the brain through the optic nerve. The eye adjusts the intensity of the light entering it by means of the iris, a diaphragm in the eye that surrounding the pupil. The iris is able to relax and contract with the help of muscles. Similar type of diaphragm in camera also adjusts the light entering in it. Similarly, the amount of light entering a camera is restricted by a device known as a diaphragm. The camera is the duplication of working mechanism of eye, decades before.

Revolution in Hearing Devices: The Fly's Ear

Hearing impaired and their problems are a burden to Government, family members. Friend s and society. To provide a better life is the prime importance under both governmental and NGOS. Hearing aids are available in the medical filed at different quality and different designs. But no one is absolutely a substitute for natural human ear and functionality. So improvement in this field is a continuous process. Thousands of research is going on all over the world to improve the hearing aids and provide better life to the hearing impaired people. Researchers are constantly searching for better hearing aids idea from nature, so that it will be better adapted to human system. One such answer is given by a tiny insect *Ormia ochracea.* Researcher hopes that the extraordinary design of the hearing organ of this fly will be revolutionize the hearing aids. The ear of this species of fly can identify the direction of sounds in a most accurate manner. The ability to locate sound in the case of human is amazing, but the distance between the two ears is about 6 or more inches. This makes a matter of differentiation of sound perceived by two ears. But in the case the fly *Ormia ochracea* the distance between two sound perceiving organs is only half a millimeter. Hence Ormia has a much bigger challenge in telling the difference. For the existence of *Ormia ochracea,* direction of sound should be indentified accurately because it must locate cricket as a food for its larvae. The *Ormia ochracea* deposit eggs atop the cricket, when the larva emerge it feeds on the cricket. *Ormia* has very sensitive ears to locate the chirping cricket. It can pinpoint sounds exceptionally well. For locating sounds, the human brain uses a similar method to that of *Ormia*. For this purpose, it's enough for sound to reach the closer ear first, then the more distant one. When a sound wave strikes the tympanum membrane, it is converted into an electrical signal and immediately transmitted to the brain. The brain analyzes the milliseconds of difference between the sound's reaching both ears and thus determines the direction it came from. The fly, whose brain is no larger than a pinhead, performs this calculation only in 50 nanoseconds, 1,000 times faster than human can do. Researchers are now trying to copy this secret in manufacturing the hearing aids and listening devices. One of such device is prepared under the trade name ORMIAFON.

Oyster Shells: Inspired Model for Light, Sturdy Roofs

Because of the irregular shape in the surface of the shell of oyster it appears wavier. This shape helps the oyster to withstand high pressure and remain very light weight. Today architect use this model to prepare many roofs to protect is from mechanical pressure and getting longevity and light weight. For example, the roof of Canada's Royan Market was designed with the oyster shell in mind. The curved surface of the oyster shell makes it especially resistant. Corrugated cardboard duplicates the curved lines found in oyster shells, making it stronger than ordinary, flat cardboard.

The Munich Olympic Stadium and Dragonfly Wings

Dragon fly a commonly both in fairy tale and in reality have wings which are one three-thousandth of a millimeter thick. But even though so thin they are very strong since they consist of up to 1,000 sections. Thanks to this compartmental structure the wings do not tear, and are able to withstand the pressure that forms during flight. The roof of the Munich Olympic Stadium was designed along the same principle.

A Structure that Makes Bones More Resistant

Even today, the Eiffel Tower is accepted as a marvel of engineering, but the event that led to its design took place back to 40 years before its construction. This was a study in Zurich aimed at revealing "the anatomical structure of the thigh bone." In the early 1850s, the anatomist Hermann von Meyer was studying the part of the thigh bone that inserts into the hip joint. The thigh bone head extends sideways into the hip socket, and bears the body's weight off-center. Von Meyer saw that the inside of the thigh bone, which is capable of withstanding a weight of one ton when in a vertical position, consists not of one single piece, but contains an orderly latticework of tiny ridges of bone known as trabecuale.

In 1866, when the Swiss engineer Karl Cullman visited von Meyer's laboratory, the anatomist von Meyer showed him a piece of bone he had been studying. Cullman realized that the bone's structure was designed to reduce the effects of weight load and pressure. The trabecuale were effectively a series of studs and braces arranged along the lines of force generated when standing. As a mathematician and engineer, Cullman translated these findings into applicable theory and the model lead to the design of the Eiffel Tower. As in the thigh bone, the Eiffel Tower's metal curves formed a lattice built from metal studs and braces. Thanks to this structure, the tower was easily able to stand up to the bending and shearing effects caused by the wind (Smithsonian-National-Zoological-Park.

The Radiolaria Design Used as a Model in Dome Design

Radiolarian and diatoms, organisms that live in the sea, are virtual catalogs of ideal solutions to architectural problems. In fact, these tiny creatures have inspired a great many large-scale architectural projects. The U.S. Pavilion at EXPO '76 in Montreal is just one example. The pavilion's dome was inspired by the radiolarians (Dr. Hanaslı Gur, 1985).

The Earthquake-Proof Design in Honeycombs

The honey comb construct impart many advantages including stability. The waggle dance performed by drons in the early morning to instruct the workers imitates a condition of earthquake. The vibrations during this dance are absorbed by the wall of the honey comb. Architect can use this model to prepare buildings to protect it from earthquake. Understanding the phase reversal will help the architect to find out the weak part of the building and correct by the architect mechanism followed by bees. Thus honey bee comb gives us new ideas which can be used to protect house, and other buildings in the areas which are more prone to earthquake. Thanks to the honey provider and highly co-ordinate sociasl insect.

Architectural Designs Drawn from Spider Webs

We have seen tarpaulin thrown over a bush, it appears like spider web. The web is prepared by this thread attached at the sides of the bush, but it cannot collapse even under light wind and rainfall. This load bearing construction help the spider spread its web and with good strength. This amazing idea is used by human to construct many structures over wide areas. The Munich Olympic Stadium, Jeddah Airport's Pilgrim Terminal, zoos in Munich and Canada, the Sydney National Athletic Stadium, Denver Airport in Colorado, and the Schlumberger Cambridge Research Centre building in England are some of the examples. This web building technique is an instinct behavior in spider and no one taught this at any way. Thanks to Mother Nature for its free amazing gift.

Robotics Is Imitating Snakes to Overcome the Problem of Balance

Equilibrium maintenance is one of the critical problem is robot construction and designing. Any robot, simple to sophisticate has face problems of balance when it begins it motion. A baby can maintain her balance with ease, but robot cannot do this are little use. Many robots prepared, one for NASA are discarded because of the lack of balance. Hence engineers always are looking the nature to get one better idea from Mother Nature. Finally they succeeded it from a reptile—Snake. Snake lacks hard spine or have flexible spine and also lack limbs. This property helps them to move through crevices with ease. They also can expand and constrict their body and can cling to branches and glide over the rocks. This property of the Snakes' inspired for a new robotic.

The Balance Center in the Inner Ear Astounds Robotics Experts

The inner ear is the organ of hearing and organ of balancing. It allows us to perform many activities even walking through tightropes without falling. This inner ear consists of three semicircular canals, arranged on orthogonal planes. This center of balance in the inner ear, known as the labyrinth, consists of three small semicircular canals. These three canals help to sense rotations in one of the three orthogonal directions. Viscous fluid is present in each of these canals. At one end of the canal contain a gelatinous cap called cupula or ampula, which sit on cristae contain sensory hair. When we turn head, or bend the fluid within these canal lags behind due to inertia. The fluid then pushes on cupula a deflecting it. This deflection is sensed by sensory hair and impulse will form and concert into electrical signaling. These signals transmitted to the brain through auditory nerve. The brain interprets and keeps balance with the help of muscles. These extraordinary processes occur in less than 1/100th of a second. Nobody created such an amazing model so far. Thanks Gold for his flawless creation.

Structure of Worm Muscles Lead the Way to New Mechanical Systems

The outer covering of worms consists of spirally wounded crossed helical structure. The contraction of the muscle cause to increase the pressure inside and the worm can change its shape and the worm become thin, long or short. This causes the worm to move. This mechanism can be transferred to some human design, for example cylinder of various fiber angles were arranged along the line of the worm's anatomy, and fill it with water absorbing gel to expand. Here chemical energy is converted into mechanical energy. If the contraction and expansion of the tube is controlled, it can be used as an artificial muscle.

Learning from Human Lungs How to Sequester-Carbon

The working of human lung is inspired to remove CO_2 form flue stacks, preventing green house gas from reaching the upper layer of atmosphere and warming, global warming. Our lung have three features which helps to remove CO_2 effectively—extremely thin surface to facilitate diffusion, extremely large surface area and specialized chemical translator namely carbonic anhydrase, which allows CO_2 to be removed from our bloodstream thousands of times faster than possible without it. A company called Carbozyme Inspired by human lungs work removed about 90% of the CO_2 traveling through flue stacks.

Learning from Nature How to Create Flow Without-Friction

Stand quietly just about anywhere and you are likely to hear a fan running—in the computer you are using, in the air conditioning unit of the building you are in, and throughout the water, air, and electrical systems upon which the city around you depends. Fans and other rotational devices are a major part of the human built environment, and a major component of our total energy usage. Although we've been building such devices in one form or another since at least 100 B.C., we've never built them like Nature does until now. Naturally flowing fluids, gases, and heat follow a common geometric pattern that differs in shape from conventional human-made rotors. Nature moves water and air using a logarithmic or exponentially growing spiral, as commonly seen in seashells. This pattern shows up everywhere in Nature: in the curled up trunks of elephants and tails of chameleons, in the pattern of swirling galaxies in outer space and kelp in ocean surf, and in the shape of the cochlea of our inner ears and our own skin pores. Inspired by the way Nature moves water and air, PAX Scientific Inc. applied this fundamental geometry to the shape of human-made rotary devices for the first time, in fans, mixers, propellers, turbines and pumps. Depending on application, the resulting designs reduce energy usage by a staggering 10-85% over conventional rotors, and noise by up to 75%.

Learning from Dolphins How to Warn People about-Tsunamis

Tsunami waves are originated in the deeper part of the ocean about 6000 meter. To know the waves and inform warning signals to the concerned nation is very difficult. Practically it is difficult because, to do this we have to plant a sensor at this depth, and connect this sensor through wire to the terminal on the land. All these crate problem in the marine environment. So scientists are always in search of natural source to solve this problem. Finally dolphins provide us a natural idea. Dolphins are able to perceive the sound of an individual (Signature whistle) up to 25 km away. This proves that dolphins are very excellent in communication through harsh media of marine environment. By many experiment, it become clear that dolphins can capture the sound in any scattered form. By imitating this ability of dolphin a company called EvoLogic has developed a high performance underwater modem for data transmission. This modem is currently used for early warning of tsunami in Indian Ocean.

Learning From Chimpanzees How to Heal Ourselves

Near about 25 % percent of medicines used today are derived from plants and plants sources. To derive medicine from plants is not a day's work; it needs thousands of year's observation, practice and practical application and its study on failure and success. Our ancestors know it better and they shown us many medicines both ayurvedic and allopathic. They did it constant observation to the animals which eating for various purpose and trial and error mechanism. By observing the domesticated animals around us we can see that these animals use or eat some vegetable when they are ill. Chimpanzee regularly uses vernonia plants leaf whenever they fall illness. This tree leaves contain a chemical which helps the chimp to cure parasitic infections like pinworm, hookworm and giardia; hence this is safe to human consumption also in humans.

Create Sustainable-Buildings: Learning from Termites

The most disturbing pest may be the termite. But termite teaches us to construct a self sustained building. Eastgate, an office complex building in Harare, Zimbabwe, is the product of termite mount secret. This building is air-conditioned but energy cost is zero. How it possible? is the lesson taught by a termite hill, constructed by *Macrotermes michaelseni*, it maintain the temperature inside the termite hill at 1°C throughout the day and night, but the temperature outside may be 40°C and above. This saves money, electricity and pollution. Let us hope that all the building in the future will construct like this and we will live in a world of zero energy crises.

Ever-sharp urchin teeth may yield tools that never need honing

Sea-urchin a bowl shaped globular echindermate live in rocky seashores where frequent tumult of waves and other predators. It has to hide themselves in nooks on rocks and protect from crashing surface. The urchins carve the rock to make its abode. The rock carving behavior of the urchin is amazing. The biomimicry interest lies in the affinity of rock boring behaviors and the teeth used never and ever faded. This mechanism can be applied to make a weapon which never has to sharpen and remain sharpened forever. The sea urchin teeth are made up of calcite crystal with plates and fibers. These plates and fibers are arranged crosswise and glued together with super hard calcite nanocement. In between the crystals are present organic materials which allow the growth of the teeth continuously. The crystal found in the urchin teeth is different from other crystals found in the nature because it has no facets and in every deepest level has orderly arranged atoms and make it mosaic pattern. It is said that the teeth of gnawing animals like rat also has a continuously growing incisor teeth, but the structure is different.

Hercules beetle: Humidity changes exoskeleton color

The horny forewing, elytra, of the beetle Hercules has the ability to change its colour from black to greenish yellow and back again to black within a few minutes. This kind of forward and reversible colour change was very rare or unknown in the insect world. The beetle *Aspidomorpha, Coptocyclia* and many other can change the colour of their elytra by changing the amount of water in the waxy layer-cuticle and their by thickness of the thin film which is responsible for the colour interference. It is observed that the dry elytra of the Hercules beetle, *Dynastes Hercules,* appears faint green in dry environment and turn black in high humid weather automatically. Electron microscopic study reveals that this green color is due to the widely open porous layer present about 3µm under the cuticle layer. This layer is three dimensional and arranged parallel to the cuticle layer. New scanning electron images, spectrophotometric measurements and physical modeling are used to unveil the mechanism of this coloration switch. The visible dry-state greenish coloration originates from a widely open porous layer located 3µm below the cuticle surface. The backscattering produced by this layer will lost when ware imbibe the structure during humid weather and weakens the diference in the refractive index.

Filter feeding basking shark inspires more efficient hydroelectric turbine

The bumpy protrusion son the flippers of whale is an inspiration to design a more efficient tidal and wind power turbines. The basking shark, a filter feeder engulf water while it moving forward through its open mouth. This water went out through the gill slits present on either side. The interesting fact is that the shark must remain as filter feeder otherwise it could not swim properly and the life of the basking shark, the largest kind among the shark become difficult and may leads to extinction. The reason for this observation is that when the shark move forward with expanded fins the water pressure under the body and fins remain greater along the straight bottom. At the same time the curved upper surface of the body increase the distance of the water to travel. This results in decreasing pressure at the top of the shark's body i.e. around the gill slits. This decreasing pressure around the gills helps to draw out the water through the gills. Hence through the evolution the shark remain as filter feeder even though it is the biggest kind in the sea. Thus in basking shark the water and enter and flow out purely passive method without expenditure of energy. In other sharks the water enters actively by suction force. This mechanism inspire engineers to construct "Straight Power" turbine in water enter through first opening and the second opening like shark's gill compress the water and make low pressure area to draw through and produce more energy.

Eiffel Tower comes from the thigh bone.

Eiffel Tower, one of the Seven Wonders of the World, erected in 1889 at Champ de Mars in Paris is an iron lattice tower. It was named after Gustave Eiffel and is the tallest structure in Paris having 324 meters height (1063 ft). It is the strongest and most solid tower in the world and is resistant to the strongest winds and shock. It is fascinating to know how the tower got all these. The tower is built by getting inspiration from our thigh bone. Herman von Meyer studied the property of the femur and found that thigh bone is capable of supporting dozens of pound without causing any crash. This is because its structure is like cage-related bars. Swiss engineer, Karl Cullman in 1866 find out that this cage-related bar structure can withstand any pressure and itself will reduce the impact of pressure applied on it. The weight reducing property is due to the fact the bars remain along the lines of force that appear when standing. Eiffel tower is also built with bars like a cage, as it appears in the lattice anatomy of the femur bone. This proves that biomimetics originate hundreds of years before, now flourishing and never perish.

CHAPTER-5

Biomimicry research

Nanotechnologists, marine biologists and signal-processing experts from Rice University, the Marine Biological Laboratory in Woods Hole, Mass., and other US universities have won $6 million from the Office of Naval Research to unlock the secrets of nature's best camouflage artists. Ultimately, the team hopes to create "metamaterials"—materials that blur the line between material and device—to emulate the elegant colors and patterns that are produced by squid and other marine animals. Mimicking the reflective iridescence of a butterfly's wing, investigators have developed a color-changing patch that could be worn on soldiers' helmets and uniforms to indicate the strength of exposure to blasts from explosives in the field. Future studies aim to calibrate the color change to the intensity of exposure to provide an immediate read on the potential harm to the brain and the subsequent need for medical intervention. Lessons learned from the ocean's largest mammals have inspired United States Naval Academy researchers to tackle one of the serious design challenges facing a technology that uses underwater turbines to convert ocean tides into electricity—work present today at the American Physical Society's Division of Fluid Dynamics (DFD) meeting in Long Beach, Calif. Working at a crossroad between biology and engineering, scientists have modeled and are now mimicking the ingenious natural design of falling geckos, gliding snakes, cruising seagulls, flapping insects and floating maple seeds to improve the design of air vehicles

Hummingbirds rank among the world's most accomplished hovering animals, but how do they manage it in gusty winds? A team of researchers has built a robotic hummingbird wing to discover the answer, which they describe today at the American Physical Society Division of Fluid Dynamics meeting in Long Beach, Calif. A team of scientists at Harvard University has reproduced many of the characteristics of real bird song with a simple physical model made of a rubber tube—work presented today at the American Physical Society Division of Fluid Dynamics meeting in Long Beach, Calif.

To avoid some of the design challenges involved in creating micro-scale air vehicles that mimic the flapping of winged insects or birds, Georgia Tech researchers propose using flexible wings that are driven by a simple sinusoidal flapping motion Airplanes do not look much like birds, but should they? This question is exactly what a pair of engineers in California and South Africa inadvertently answered recently in experiments they describe today at the American Physical Society Division of Fluid Dynamics meeting in Long Beach, Calif Scientists at the University of Southampton have developed a new kind of underwater sonar device that can detect objects through bubble clouds that would effectively blind standard sonar

Researchers at Case Western Reserve University use two high-speed cameras and a computer program they developed to quickly and accurately analyze the simultaneous movement of all 26 leg joints in a walking cockroach. They have made the program free and open-source for other insect researchers to use

Scientists at the University of Maryland and Tulane University have developed a computational model of a swimming fish that is the first to address the interaction of internal and external forces on locomotion. The research team simulated how the fish's body bends, depending on the forces from the fluid moving around it as well as the muscles inside. Understanding these interactions will help design medical prosthetics for humans that work with the body's natural mechanics

Geckos have amazingly sticky feet. Their stick ability comes from billions of dry microscopic hairs that coat the soles of their feet. However, when humidity increases, gecko feet stick even tighter to smooth surfaces, so how do they do it? Kellar Autumn and his colleagues have found that increased humidity softens the keratin that makes up the sticky foot-hairs, allowing them to deform and stick tighter to surfaces than hairs in dry conditions

The University of Washington is leading a five-year, $7.5 million project to study birds, insects and bats in order to develop autonomous aerial vehicles that can adapt to obstacles and fly in unpredictable conditions

A team led by a North Carolina State University researcher has shown that water-gel-based solar devices—"artificial leaves"—can act like solar cells to produce electricity. The findings prove the concept for making solar cells that more closely mimic nature. They also have the potential to be less expensive and more environmentally friendly than the current standard-bearer: silicon-based solar cells

Geckos are masters at sticking to surfaces of all kinds and easily un-sticking themselves. Inspired by these lizards, a team of engineers has developed a reversible adhesion method for printing electronics on a variety of tricky surfaces such as clothes, plastic and leather. Designed by researchers from Northwestern University and the University of Illinois at Urbana-Champaign, the stamp easily can pick up electronic devices from a silicon surface and print them on a curved surface

Most bio-inspired robots have been based on animals with jointed, stiff skeletons. There is now an increasing interest in mimicking the robust performance of animals in natural environments by incorporating compliant materials into the locomotory system. However, the mechanics of moving, highly conformable structures are particularly difficult to predict. This paper proposes a planar, extensible-link model for the soft-bodied tobacco hornworm caterpillar, *Manduca sexta*, to provide insight for biologists and engineers studying locomotion by highly deformable animals and caterpillar-like robots. Using inverse dynamics to process experimentally acquired point-tracking data, ground reaction forces and internal forces were determined for a crawling caterpillar. Computed ground reaction forces were compared to experimental data to validate the model. The results show that a system of linked extendable joints can faithfully describe the general form and magnitude of the contact forces produced by a crawling caterpillar. Furthermore, the model can be used to compute internal forces that cannot be measured experimentally. It is predicted that between different body segments in stance phase the body is mostly kept in tension and that compression only occurs during the swing phase when the pro-legs release their grip. This finding supports a recently proposed mechanism for locomotion by soft animals in which the substrate transfers compressive forces from one part of the body to another (the environmental skeleton) thereby minimizing the need for hydrostatic stiffening. The model also provides a new means to characterize and test control strategies used in caterpillar crawling and soft robot locomotion. (Frank Saunders *et al*, 2011).

Here we demonstrate the feasibility of using an array of live insects to detect concentrated packets of odor and infer the location of an odor source (~15 m away) using a backward Lagrangian dispersion model based on the Langevin equation. Bayesian inference allows uncertainty to be quantified, which is useful for robotic planning. The electro antennogram (EAG) is the bio-potential developed between the tissue at the tip of an insect antenna and its base, which is due to the massed response of the olfactory receptor neurons to an odor stimulus. The EAG signal can carry tens of bits per second of information with a rise time as short as 12 ms (Justice, 2005). Here, instrumentation including a GPS with a digital compass and an ultrasonic 2D anemometer has been integrated with an EAG odor detection scheme, allowing the location of an odor source to be estimated by collecting data at several downwind locations. Bayesian inference in conjunction with a Lagrangian dispersion model, taking into account detection errors, has been implemented resulting in an estimate of the odor source location within 0.2 m of the actual location. (Myrick and Baker, 2011).

Unlike the falling cat, lizards can right themselves in mid-air by a swing of their large tails in one direction causing the body to rotate in the other. Here, we developed a new three-dimensional analytical model to investigate the effectiveness of tails as inertial appendages that change body orientation. We anchored our model using the morphological parameters of the flat-tailed house gecko *Hemidactylus platyurus*. The degree of roll in air righting and the amount of yaw in mid-air turning directly measured in house geckos matched the model's results. Our model predicted an increase in body roll and turning as tails increase in length relative to the body. Tails that swung from a near orthogonal plane relative to the body (i.e. 0-30° from vertical) were the most effective at generating body roll, whereas tails operating at steeper angles (i.e. 45-60°) produced only half the rotation. To further test our analytical model's predictions, we built a bio-inspired robot prototype. The robot reinforced how effective attitude control can be attained with simple movements of an inertial appendage. (Jusufi *et al* 2010)

Thermal soaring saves much energy, but flying large distances in this form represents a great challenge for birds, people and unmanned aerial vehicles (UAVs). The solution is to make use of the so-called thermals, which are localized, warmer regions in the atmosphere moving upward with a speed exceeding the descent rate of birds and planes. Saving energy by exploiting the environment more efficiently is an important possibility for autonomous UAVs as well. Successful control strategies have been developed recently for UAVs in simulations and in real applications. This paper first presents an overview of our knowledge of the soaring flight and strategy of birds, followed by a discussion of control strategies that have been developed for soaring UAVs both in simulations and applications on real platforms.

To improve the accuracy of the simulation of thermal exploitation strategies we propose a method to take into account the effect of turbulence. Finally, we propose a new GPS-independent control strategy for exploiting thermal updrafts. (Zsuzsa Ákos *et al*, 2010).

We propose to design a small-size transmission-coupled antenna array, and corresponding radiation pattern, having high performance inspired by the female *Ormia ochracea*'s coupled ears. For reproduction purposes, the female *Ormia* is able to locate male crickets' call accurately despite the small distance between its ears compared with the incoming wavelength. This phenomenon has been explained by the mechanical coupling between the *Ormia*'s ears, which has been modeled by a pair of differential equations. In this paper, we first solve these differential equations governing the *Ormia ochracea*'s ear response, and convert the response to the pre-specified radio frequencies. We then apply the converted response of the biological coupling in the array factor of a uniform linear array composed of finite-length dipole antennas, and also include the undesired electromagnetic coupling due to the proximity of the elements. Moreover, we propose an algorithm to optimally choose the biologically inspired coupling for maximum array performance. In our numerical examples, we compute the radiation intensity of the designed system for binomial and uniform ordinary end-fire arrays, and demonstrate the improvement in the half-power beam width, side lobe suppression and directivity of the radiation pattern due to the biologically inspired coupling. (Murat Akçakaya and Arye Nehorai, 2010).

The Wyoming Information, Signal Processing, and Robotics Laboratory is developing a wide variety of bio-inspired vision sensors. We are interested in exploring the vision system of various insects and adapting some of their features toward the development of specialized vision sensors. We do not attempt to supplant traditional digital imaging techniques but rather develop sensor systems tailor made for the application at hand. We envision that many applications may require a hybrid approach using conventional digital imaging techniques enhanced with bio-inspired analogue sensors. In this specific project, we investigated the apposition compound eye and its characteristics commonly found in diurnal insects and certain species of arthropods. We developed and characterized an array of apposition compound eye-type sensors and tested them on an autonomous robotic vehicle. The robot exhibits the ability to follow a pre-defined target and avoid specified obstacles using a simple control algorithm. (Davis *et al,* 2009).

Nano-structured colorful zinc oxide (ZnO) replicas were produced using the wings of the *Ideopsis similis* butterfly as templates. The ZnO replicas we obtained exhibit iridescence, which was clearly observed under an optical microscope (OM). Field emission scanning electron microscope analysis shows that all the microstructure details are maintained faithfully in the ZnO replica. A computer model was established to simulate the diffraction spectral results, which agreed well with the OM images. (Wang Zhang *et al,* 2006).

Teeth reveal evolution:
From the horse's mouth

Paleodentists excavated fossilized horse teeth of about 55.5. Million years ago and reported the timeline of changing the features of teeth according to the climate change in the past. Horse diet changed in a massive way during its evolution and the change in diet reflected in the pattern and structure of teeth of the horse. The pattern of change in teeth structure shows that horse was fruiting in the past and changed to grazing one later.

Earlier microscopic wear method was used to study the structure of teeth and its evolution in the past. But this method requires more precision and hard labor work and is very sophisticated. Hence this method can be applied to a limited number of animals and also in a limited period of time. To minimize all these shortcomings a new approach is employing today known as mesowear. The mesowear method purely relies on the shape of the teeth, particularly on the sharpness of the cusps of molars. This method allows the researcher to study large number of specimen in a short period of time and also with more precision. The fruit eating behavior need a pattern of teeth now observing in monkeys, tarsiuers and lorises, but grazing behavior needs teeth with somewhat more flat ns narrow cusps. When the researcher analyzed past horse teeth in the fissile and today's horse teeth it become very evident that the hortse evolved from fruit eating habit to more grazing one.

The history of horse's teeth evolution

North America is the place where horse originated. But the horse species extinct here about 10,000 years ago after some migrated to other continents. Later they horse returned to America again through European Explorers and Colonists. It is estimated that the first horse in North America emerged before 55.5 Million years ago. At the beginning the horse was small in size like a fox with small crowned teeth. Their round cusps in molar revealed that they were lived by eating fruits in warm, forested, moist climate. The horse's teeth changed since about 33 Million years ago. The teeth become sharper pointes, an adaptation for leaf eating behavior. Around this time the climate become colder due to the disappearance of rain forest.

The result of fossil study and their comparison with the present horse teeth given a consistent result showing the horse's teeth changed over the time with change in climate pattern. The surface of their molar become more complex and better adapted for grazing and chewing hard and tough materials like grass. The grass cell wall is impregnated with silica and hence it needs sharper and stronger teeth to cut and tear. The height of the teeth also had grown gradually during this evolution. All these changes are correlated with change in grass land pattern d forest pattern, a very good example for Darwin's natural selection and evolution. The story of the horse evolution is not ended with this, since last 10 Million years ago the intermediate diet totally disappeared and a horse with highly abrasive, grassy diet evolved.

But the question still remain why the horse left the fruit eating behavior, it may be only due to the mass destruction of forest by natural calamities, a frequent occurrence in the past.

Tree frog with behavior of self cleaning feet Inspired New Medicine.

Tree frog has sticky pads on their toes. This pad is used to cling on tree branches. If nay dirt is stick on the pad it will trouble the frog to perform its sole function of clinging. Hence the animal keeps the surface of the pad clean. How the frog keep it clean a mystery for decades. Recently it is explored that the frog secretes mucus to make the pad sticky. The frog used this mucus to clean the pad by rubbing on the surface. If this secrete is transferred into man-made adhesive it could provide reusable, pollution free, nontoxic

Chapter-6

Biomimicry: In Molecular Level

Biomaterial

An important application in the field of biomimetics is the use of biomaterials. This involves mimicking or synthesizing natural substances to apply in practical design. Now days to site example for biomaterials is immense, each having unique properties. The biomaterials are biodegradable, the most important property of biomaterial. Beside this, the biomaterial does not need high temperature and sophisticated machinery to prepare. This leads to a pollution free technology and process.

Spider silk

The silk produced by spider is one of the most widely studied biomaterial. This material is secreted by special glands in the distal portion of spider. It is light, flexible and many times stronger than steel, for example the tensile strength of steel is 400Mpa and that of spider silk is only 1154Mpa. (Vogel, Steven, 2003). The web os spider silk contain two forms, an ampulated silk for drags line and web frame, the second one is viscid silk for gluing the silk (*Gosline, 1999*).

It is a common observation that when a flying insect caught in the web of a spider it slows its motion and finally halts this due to the absorption of kinetic energy of the flying insect by the web *(Gosline, 1999)*. The web damage during this capturing of flying insect is by lengthening the time for slows down the flying insect. When it take long time for slows down smaller the force needed for top it i.e. reducing the potential energy and their by reduce the damage to the web. The unusual properties of the spider silk are due to its molecular structure (Fig1). Studies by X-ray diffraction methods reveals that the silk is composed of a long chain of amino acids which forming crystal; lattice. The major part of h silk is formed by beet sheets crystals formed by tandemly repeated small amino acid residues *(Gosline, 1999)*. It is analyzed that the amino acid sequence is made up of 8-20 poly-alanin and 24-35 glycine residues. The beet-sheet formed by these amino acid residues are then cross linked by fibroin protein and forming a polymer, which forming a net work imparting great stiffness, toughness and strength. This crystalline structure is present in rubbery structure formed by 16-20 amino acid residues long. This structure gives extensibility and tensile strength to the fiber. This special property along with light weight enables the silk to withstand during wind and remain without pulled off from its anchoring pint. These properties make the spider silk more demandable; hence some commercial companies turn its attention towards this line recently. Nexia biotechnology is a firm in Quebec. This firm succeeded in introducing silk genes of two spiders in the milk gland of transgenic goat *(Atkins, 2003)*. Researcher precipitated the silk from the milk in the form of web like material and named it

Biosteel (*Atkins, 2003*). This technology can be used in medicine to prepare tough, strong, ligaments, tendons, and limbs. It also used in wound healing, tissue repair nano biodegradable, materials for eye or neurosurgery and substitute for Kevlar (Benyus, Janine, 1997).

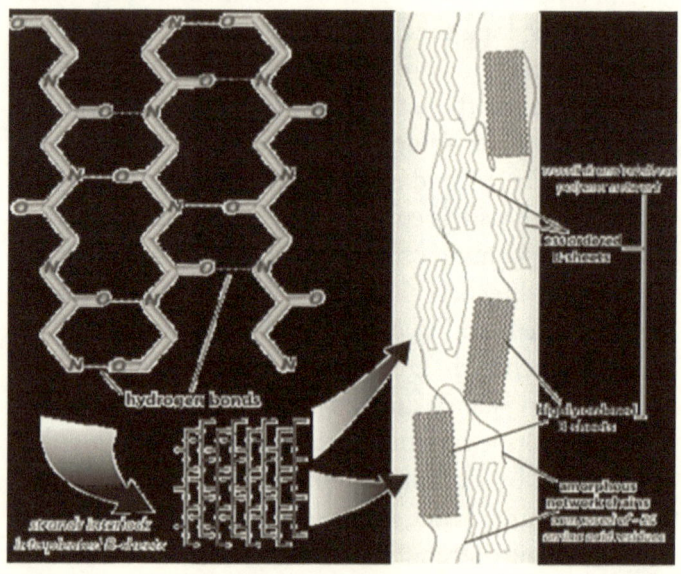

The structure of a strand of silk

Primary structure

Bioinformatics' analysis of the sequence of spider silk prove that it is rich in protein containing non-polar and hydrophobic amino acids like glycine or alanine, but tryptophan is totally lacking (Ashokan. And Pillai, 2008. Spider silk protein is different from other protein due to its aberrant nature and highly repetitive sequence of amino acid; about 90% and short polypeptide stretch only 10-50%. These domains repeated many times and impart special structural properties like strength, flexibility and toughness. (Lewi, 2006). For example in MAP and Flag silks contain about four oligopeptide domain which are repeated many times: [I] (GA)n/(A)n, [II] GPGGX/GPGQQ, [III] GGX (X = A, S or Y) and [IV] "spacer" sequences which contain charged amino acids (Hayashi AND Lewis,1998 and 2001). It is also shown that the oligopeptides with the sequence (GA)n/(A)n form α-helices in solution and β-sheet structures in assembled fibers (van Beek,2002 Simmon *et al*, 1996). The structures formed by oligopeptides with the sequences GPGGX/GPGQQ and GGX have not identified so far. Several studies describe these regions to adopt amorphous rubber-like structures (Gosline *et al*, 1994; Termonia, 1994). While others suggest formation of a 31-helical structure(van Beek *et al,*, 2002). Flabelliform silk is typically rich in GPGGX and GGX motifs which folds into β-turn structures resulting in a right-handed β-spiral helix on stacking (Hayashi and Lewis, 1998 Becker *et al*, 2003). The non-repetitive regions are located at the protein's termini (Scheibel, 2005). The non repetitive motifs are responsible for the formation fiber like structure. This domain contain about 100-200 amino acid resides which helps to form secondary and tertiary in solutioin(Rising, 2006. Sponner *et al*, 2005). These domains are interconnected by disulphide bonds and maintain the dimer and multimers under oxidized condition. Hence these domains are responsible for assembly of silk proteins (Sponner *et al*, 2005; 2004 Huemmerich, 2004). The carboxy terminal and repetitive sequence of different silk were identified and reveals ahigh degree of homology between them (Rising, 2006; Hu X,, 2006. Motriuk-Smith, 2005*)*. One full length sequence of a Flag silk protein of Nephila *clavipes* having both termini is identified so far. Similarly the first full length sequence of MA silk fiber of black widow spider has been reported. The Flag silk gene is lack introns but consisting large exons (>9,000 bp of coding sequence). The large exons are due to the gene duplication during evolution. It is observed that, genes with shorter introns show a higher expression rate than genes with large introns (Castillo-Davis, 2002). The spider silks are highly expressed throughout the lifetime of the spider. Hydrophobic and hydrophilic domains are alternately repeat in spider silk, a character of primary structure. This amphiphilic constitution is thought to be a reminiscent of surfactants or biological membranes and is thought to be crucial for phase separation during the spinning process (Exler *et al*, 2007; Hermanson *et al*, 2007; Jin AND Kaplan, 2003). This amphiphilic antute is also responsible for micelles formation, an intermediate structure formed during fiber (Vollrath and Knight, 2001).

Quaternary structure and protein stability.

When the silk is secreted it appears as solution and is lack of secondary or tertiary structure. (Riekel *et al*, 1999). When this soluble protein pass through the spinning ducts the repetitive sequence of the silk interact with nearby domain and got secondary and tertiary structure that present in the natural silk. We can identify the area of high electron density embedded areas with low electron density are by using Roentgen diffraction analysis of the final structure of MA silk threads (Kaplan *et al*, 1993; Fraser and MacRae, 1973; Gosline *et al*, 1992). It is observed that the high electron density regions comprise high β-sheet content, substructure (Kubik, 2002*)*. The mechanical strength of the silk is due to these sub-structures. Research finding alos shows that the elasticity of the fiber is due to its low electron density area, which is amorphous with few secondary or no secondary structures (Hayashi *et al*, 1999). This type structure resembles the hydrogel (Rammensee *et al*, 2006). When the thread is under tensile loading, the hydrogel area deform and providing the elasticity and flexibility to the thread. The different composition of crystalline and hydrogel can cause the formation of different silk threads. The MAP used for the construction of web contains more β-sheet. Silk, which is more flexible contain more hydrogel areas and is amorphous. It shows the structure and function of the silk protein is closely associated with its structure. But it has to substantiate in the future research.

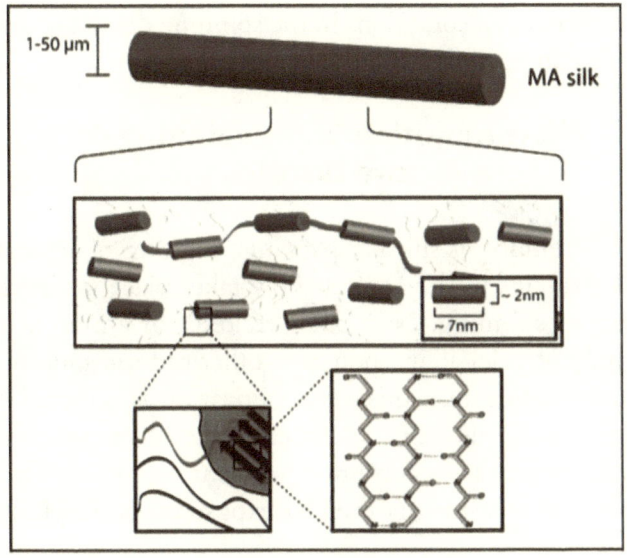

Structure of MAP silk

The Assembly of Spider Silk Starting with a highly concentrated spinning dope

In the case of spider silk protein the assembly of protein the assembly is not start with folded globular protein monomers, but with unfolded intrinsic proteins at high concentration. (Dicko *et al*, 2004). Many factors are responsible for maintaining high protein concentration, up to 50% v/v (Hijirida *et al*, 1996). In the silk gland, including liquid crystallinity, lyotropic, glycosylation of the folded silk proteins and phase separation by a polyol or by a phospholipids surfactant (SenGupta *et al*, 2007). Random coiling start at beginning and then passing through the tubes of the gland, as it pass through, it assemble itself and become water—insoluble (Scheibe, 2004). This assembly needs bi-stable folding of the protein and control of the environmental conditions in the spinning duct (e.g., pH, ionic concentration, water content).

Phase transition in the spinning duct: two theories.

Assembly of silk i.e. packing, aligning of separate silk proteins in the laminar flow takes place inside the duct of spinning. Non polar residues of amino acids (Hydrophobic) align upon each other to form multimer (Multimerization), this multimerization is initiated by the terminal domains and shear force in the spinning duct. Hence theses polyamine segment is exposed. These polyalanine segments thereby expose on hydrophobic surface which stimulate the formation of β-sheet structure having many inter and intra-chain hydrogen bonds the formation (Scheibe, 2004).

Presently, researchers proposed two theories for the mechanism of assembly of silk fibers in spider silk (Jin and Kaplan, 2003; Iekel *et al*, 1999; Ko and Jovicic, 2004). The first one is the crystalline alignment of the underlying proteins in the laminar flow inside the spinning duct. Monomers are aligned lengthwise and form mulitmers, which then n linked by disulphide bond for stability while it passing through spinning duct. The spinning dope attain liquid crystalline like behavior by aligning the monomers in one direction Because of this liquid crystal like state force like vander-Walals and hydrogen bond formation between nearby (Iekel *et al*, 1999). By further dehydration the silk fiber conversion completed and the fiber drawn out of the spinnerets. The second model explains micelle theory; in which silk protein first assemble in the form micelles. The micelles are formed due to amphiphilic properties inside the spinning dope (Jin and Kaplan, 2003). A grupo of such micelles form globules. When the glubules passing through the spinning duct it elongates by the sheer force applying on them and is finally the thread emerging out of the spinning tube.

Mechanical properties of spider silk.

Maximal resilience is the most outstanding property of spider silk. The spider threads can absorb three times more energy than steel (Kubik, 2002). Synthetic fibers always more stiff when compare to the natural one. Natural fibers are more flexible. For example synthetic fibers have a yield point at approx 4 GPa i.e. five times more than the best natural silk fibers. The synthetic fiber will elongate and break on bending but spider silk fibers cannot hence mechanically outperform than other natural and synthetic fibers. (Vendrely C, Scheibel, 2007).

Mechanical properties of natural and synthetic fibers
(taken from refs (Hermanson *et al*, 2007; Ko and, Jovicic, 2004).)

Material	trength [Gpa]	Elasticity [%]	Toughness [MJ m^{-3}]
MA silk*	1.1	27	180
Flag silk*	0.5	270	150
Insect silk#	0.6	18	70
Nylon 6.6	0.95	18	80
Kevlar 49	3.6	2.7	50
Carbon fiber	4	1.3	25
Steel	1.5	0.8	6

*European garden spider *Araneus diadematus.*
#Silkworm *Bombyx mori.*

Another property of the spider thread is tortional shape and memory; hence prevent the spider from twisting and turning during descending on MAP silk fibers (Emile, 2006; Emile, 2007). The spider thread cannot require extra energy to recover if turned from its initial position. The spider thread has high damping coefficient hence it cannot oscillate after twisting. The contraction rate is very superior in spider silk (Liu, 2006 Perez Rigueiro *et al*, 2003). Water absorption leads to shrinkage and tightens the thread and hence is important to ensure the rigidity of the spider's web during its lifetime (Shao *et al*, 1999; Yang, 2000).

Insect silk is different from Spider silk?

Spider silk is often compared with insect silk, especially silk form silkworm *Bombyx mori*. The silkworm silk is obtained from cocoon, while spider silk is obtained from by manually drawing the silk thread out of the spinning wart of immobilized spiders. But, this process is only suitable for MA silk (and not for the other spider silks), it is highly exnesive and time consuming. The differences between insect and spider silks are evident on all levels, from the molecules involved to the structural arrangement of the proteins to the mechanical properties of the thread. On a molecular level, insect silk comprises a large amount of sericin-proteins, which are absent in spider silk. The proteins which are responsible for the fibrillar structure (so-called fibroins in insect silk) are, in contrast to spider silk spidroins, composed of light and heavy chain counterparts. Mechanically, silkworm silk is much weaker and less extensible as compared to for example MA silk of spiders. (Vollrath, 2001; Wilding and Hearle, 1996). Interestingly, depending on spinning conditions, silkworm silk is either strong or elastic, whereas spider silk combines both properties (Shao Z, Vollrath, 2002). Although the mechanical properties of both types of silk crucially depend on spinning conditions, it is primarily the proteins involved that make the real difference. Therefore, techniques have long been sought to recombinantly produce and engineer natural spider silk proteins.

Mimicking Nature

Spider silk: A recombinant product

To study the details of the structure and assembly behavior of silk protein recombinnatly produced— recombinant spider silk is essential, because recombinant method can produce large quantity of the silk in a short period of time. Determining the complete cDNA sequence of the spider silk gene is very complicated because of its highly repetitive character of the silk protein molecules. This is the reason why complete information regarding the silk gene is not available. The demerit of repetitive protein is that it gives wrong interpretation of the nature of the protein, and provides incomplete information regarding the gene size. At the beginning the recombinant spider silk protein was obtained by direct introduction of silk protein gene into a suitable vector like bacteria. This also leads to some complication as the recombinant spider silk protein in bacteria use different codons as compared to bacteria itself. To overcome this demerit eukaryotic vector like fungi, *Pichia pastoris,* were used later to express the silk genome. But the new problems aging stem up here during the purification, instead of production process. Then the next level attempts were made with plants (Potato or Tobacco), there also faced the same problems, but now these methods are more widely used due to its wide scale production of the required protein in short time.

During the last decades other transgenic expression system also practiced widely fort the spider silk gene or fragments. One of the interesting one is the expression of spider silk in the milk glands of transgenic. This experiment was done by a Canadian company Nexia Biotechnology. But the protein in the milk was found to be very less and moreover this protein to be extracted is very impossible. Similar experiment was done by using mammalian cell line with similar results. Later insect which was very closely related phylogenic aspects were used by using proper vector like baculovirus. One of the benefits this type phylogentically related organism in this line is that it easily infect the insect. cDNAs, partial, consisting of carboxyterminl repetitive of known sequence and sequence of nonrepetitive of the two MAP of ADF3, ADF4 and *Araneus diadematus* were cloned by using Baculovirus genome. This virus was then making to infect the insect line of different species like *Spodoptera frugiperda* and *Trichopulsia ni*. In these cells at the time of cytoplasmic production of this protein they remained either as soluble or as solid fibers depending on the silk protein. The use of baculovirus is advantages because it can be easily modified and cultured ad their by easily modified expression. Production on larger scale we have to select other source, baculovirus cannot help us in this sense. For this purpose the spider silk gene must be incorporated in the genome of the bacteria.

Cloning strategy is better for the large scale production of silk fiber protein by PCR method. It includes both carboxyterminal nonrepetitive region and codon optimized repetitive regions. By using cloning technique a well regulated engineered modules and authentic gene fragments or artifacts without gaps or artifacts in the genome is possible. By this method the yield also can be increased enormously. Another advantage of this method is we can engineer the protein as per our need with for experimental purpose.

Artificial spinning of spider silk.

When the recombinant spider silks are available in required quantity it is easy to analyze the various assembly of spider silk thread in a functional in vitro spinning process in the future. This process is advantageous, but it must ensure that the artificial silk will reassemble in natural silk in its chemical composition, mechanical properties and moreover its microstructures. The spinning machinery of the spider needs many aspects to be considered like protein composition of the spinning dope, many mechanical properties and phase separation process in the spinning duct. The spider's behavior of drawing threads with its hind leg should be copied in the laboratory. The spinning speed and temperature should be maintained as per the natural process. In the nature or lab condition silk produced under high reeling speed shows higher yielding, but weaker and have less extensibility than silk produced t low speed.

For scientific purpose recombinant spider silk protein is needed. Several methods can be used for this purpose like wet-spinning process; silicon micro spinnerets methods etc. micro-spinnerets method yields several meters long threads. The wet-spinning method yield thread similar to natural thread, but the thickness is many times higher hence the physical and chemical properties are low. The alternate post spinning technique employed also yield thicker threads. Now silk proteins are widely used for many novel materials like silk film, silk solution etc. The silk solution can be made to thin nano film and can be used for many experimental purpose.

On the film the proteins change to a helical structure, which on treatment with methanol resulted in rearrangement of protein structure by increasing the β-sheet content dramatically. Silk fiber can be made into nano-fibers by treatment with potassium phosphate at room temperature, and it mimics amyloidal fibers. By analyzing the structure and functional relationship of the silk protein the secret of the extra ordinary strength and load bearing capacity of the protein can expose in the near future.

Mussel adhesive

Mussels and other marine organisms secrete remarkable protein-based adhesive materials for adherence to the substrates upon which they reside. The protein adhesives are secreted as fluids that undergo an in-situ cross linking or hardening reaction leading to the formation of a solid adhesive plaque, which mediates the attachment of the organism to a variety of substrates (e.g. minerals, metal surfaces, and wood). One of the unique structural features of mussel adhesive proteins (MAPs) is the presence of L-3, 4-dihydroxyphenylalanine (DOPA), an amino acid that is believed to be responsible for both adhesive and cross linking characteristics of MAPs. DOPA is formed in these proteins by post-translational hydroxylation of tyrosine residues. Although the exact role of DOPA in these proteins is not known, recent evidence suggests that bulk oxidation of DOPA residues leads to intermolecular cross linking of the plaque proteins giving rise to solidification of the adhesive, whereas interfacial adhesion to substrates is generally believed to be due to chemical interactions between the unoxidized catechol form of DOPA and functional groups at the surface of the solid substrate. Despite extensive studies conducted by Herbert Waite and others that have led to an increased understanding of these remarkable natural adhesives, there remains an incomplete understanding of their adhesive and cohesive mechanisms. Furthermore, mussel adhesive mimetic polymers have not been extensively developed for medical applications.

Our group is actively developing synthetic polymers that mimic the composition and properties of adhesive proteins found in nature. We have several projects whose goals are 1) to employ molecular-level adhesion experiments to gain a detailed understanding of the role of DOPA in biological adhesion; and 2) to use this information to motivate the design of new DOPA-containing macromolecular biomaterials. For example, in one project DOPA containing peptides are being incorporated into biocompatible polymers for potential use as adhesive biomaterials. To facilitate the solid phase synthesis of DOPA-containing peptides for this project, we developed a new Fmoc-DOPA (Ceof) building block, which we used to synthesize a decapeptide motif derived from a mussel adhesive protein (Tetrahedron Letetr, vol.41 2000, 5795-598). Our initial approach was to design gel-forming polymers consisting of single DOPA residues coupled to the end groups of linear and branched PEGs(Biomacromolecules, vol.3, 2002, 1038-1047).), which rapidly polymerized into hydrogels upon addition of enzymatic and chemical oxidizers. There is some evidence in the literature that the unoxidized (catechol) form of DOPA is more adhesive to metal oxide surfaces than oxidized forms of DOPA. Although adhesion experiments designed to test this hypothesis are underway (collaboration with the Shull group), we have also been exploring the design of DOPA-containing polymers that have the ability to solidify without relying upon oxidation of DOPA. Our first effort in this area was to couple DOPA residues to the end groups of ABA type block copolymers, and to take advantage of thermal gelation of aqueous solutions of these polymers. DOPA-containing PEO-PPO-PEO block copolymers were synthesized, and aqueous solutions of these polymers were found to undergo a sol-gel transition when warmed from ambient to body temperature (Biomolecules, Vol.3, 2002, 397-4060).

To the best of our knowledge, this was the first report of a DOPA-containing polymer that is capable of gelling in the absence of oxidizing agents. In the same paper, we demonstrated that the introduction of DOPA significantly increased the adhesive interactions of the block copolymers to mucin, a major macromolecular component of mucosal membranes. We also exploring the use of transglutaminase enzymes to crosslink DOPA-c ontaining peptide modified polymers into hydrogels (Jpurnal of the American Chemical Society, vol.125, 2003, 14298-14299). More information can be found in the section on Injectable biomaterials and Tissue Engineering.

More recently, we have been designing DOPA mimetic monomers capable of polymerization by free radical or atom transfer radical polymerization (ATRP) methods. In a recent paper, N-methacrylated DOPA monomers were synthesized and copolymerized with PEG diacrylate by ultraviolet and visible light to form hydrogels (Lee J. Biomaterials Science

Paper 2004). To our knowledge, this is the first report of a DOPA-containing hydrogel formed by photopolymerization. Despite a retarding inhibitory effect of DOPA on photopolymerization,

DOPA-containing monomers were successfully incorporated into PEG hydrogels. A contact mechanical test was performed on the photocured gels and the elastic moduli were obtained by fitting the load-displacement data using a Hertzian relationship, demonstrating that the gels possess moduli sufficient for use in many biomedical applications. Controlled polymerization techniques such as ATRP are also being explored for synthesis of DOPA containing polymer hydrogels. Experiments aimed at determining the adhesive properties of these hydrogels are underway. The resulting hydrogels do not require oxidizing reagents to gel; the incorporation of DOPA into hydrogels in the unoxidized state may prove to be an important tool in further understanding the role of DOPA in mussel adhesive proteins and may lead to new adhesive hydrogels for biomedical applications. Finally, we are also utilizing mussel adhesive protein mimetic peptides to anchor nonfouling polymers onto surfaces for control of biointerfaces. More information on this project can be found in the section on Biointerface/ Biofouling Research.

Formaldehyde-free eyelash glue developed from mussel adhesive protein

The MAP based bioadhesive formulation offers a non-toxic, irritant-free alternative to the use of formaldehyde in eylash glue applications,

Dr Scarmoutzos, President and CEO of Kollodis BioSciences, told Cosmetics Design. Formaldehyde is added as a preservative to cosmetic adhesives, and although approved for use in such products, it may cause contact dermatitis in people with sensitive skin. Despite the use of formaldehyde in cosmetic glues being regulated, Dr Scarmoutzos believes some products may contain higher levels than allowed. "Most government agencies regulate the level of formaldehyde exposure in humans (currently at about a 20 ppm upper limit). But that hasn't stopped some unscrupulous distributors and marketers of (eyelash glue) products containing illegally high levels of toxic formaldehyde."

Mussel adhesive protein is a unique compound found in the sticky glue secreted by the foot of the common mussel that anchors it to rocks and other objects. Kollodis 'proprietary recombinant adhesive protein, a core ingredient in its compositions, is derived from the Mediterranean mussel. According to Kollodis, mussel adhesive proteins have long been recognized as being biocompatible, environmentally friendly, and effective bioadhesives for a wide variety of applications including consumer and cosmetic applications. Dr Scarmoutzos said that although several other companies offer mussel adhesive protein products, he believes Kollodis to be the first company to use MAP technology in cosmetic glues. In accordance with the agreement, Lifeace will fund the development and commercialization of cosmetic glue products which use Kollodis' proprietary MAP technology. The company will also acquire the intellectual property for formaldehyde-free eyelash glue applications as well as options to acquire additional products that are developed as a result of the collaboration. Discussing alternative uses of the mussel adhesive proteins, Dr Scarmoutzos said that several potential applications are being considered, including an anti-acne facial mask.

"Our mussel adhesive protein has shown excellent antimicrobial activity when recombinantly coupled with antimicrobial peptides. We have an anti-acne peptide candidate which we plan to further develop for this application," he said.

Mussel adhesive for DNA chips

Mussels are true masters of adhesion. Whether on the wood of a pier, the metal of a ship's hull, rocks, or to their own kind, they stick to everything. Researchers led by Philip B. Messersmith at Northwestern University (Evanston, IL/USA) have successfully synthesized a mimic of one of the "universal adhesives "used by mussels. As the scientists report in the journal *Angewandte Chemie*, they were able to use their synthetic "mussel glue" to fix DNA molecules on various substrates. This new, simple method seems particularly promising for the production of DNA chips for diagnostics and research.

Mussel adhesive: rust protection of the future?

Mussels´ ability to attach themselves to various materials may offer the environment-friendly way of providing rust protection in the future. Corrosion of metals, such as rust, is expensive for society. In the USA alone, the estimated bill is USD 350 billion a year (approximately EUR 267bn).

Hazardous

The corrosion process, which is natural, goes on all around us. It cannot be stopped, but it can be slowed down. Traditionally, 'corrosion inhibitors' are used to reduce the rate of corrosion and thereby reduce the damage. These are effective, but many are also hazardous to health and the environment. The chromate process is one example. In cooperation with the company Biopolymer Products AB in Gothenburg, five researchers at the Royal Institute of Technology in Stockholm (KTH)—Jinshan Pan, Per Claesson, Andra Dėdinaitė, Fan Zhang and Olga Krivosheeva—have come up with an environment-friendly alternative to the chromate process, which is hazardous to health and the environment.

Composed of proteins

The alternative was found in the blue mussel. This animal has the ability to cling to virtually every material by making 'byssal threads' (the 'byssus'), which it attaches to underwater substrates. The mussel's unique means of adhesion, i.e. the thread, permits attachment even to surfaces with such low surface energy as wax and Teflon®. A bioadhesive material composed of proteins, the byssus also has an unusual capability to repel water from a surface while attaching itself to the surface and hardening under water. Mussel adhesive protein (MAP) also has the ability to form film that protects materials against corrosion.'We have a patent-protected production method for MAP, which is one of the key components in the adhesive film;' says Björn Strandwitz, CEO of Biopolymer Products AB.

Advanced technology

The KTH research team has used advanced surface-sensitive techniques to evaluate how rapidly the molecules attach to the surface (adsorption kinetics), how the protective film is formed and how far the corrosion rate is reduced (corrosion inhibition) by means of mussel protein. The scientists have also looked at how these properties are affected by the mussels´ surroundings, such as the ambient water salinity and pH value. Their findings show that MAP adsorbs rapidly and forms stable films that markedly slow down corrosion within a large pH interval. 'In-situ AFM microscopy and electrochemical measurements of carbon steel in saline water show that MAP adsorbs on carbon steel across a broad pH interval, and that it forms a carbon film that covers the whole substrate and thickens over time,´ says Professor Jinshan Pan at KTH. This means that the MAP can effectively protect carbon steel from rusting. Björn Strandwitz adds: 'Carbon steel is one of the commonest materials in, for example, steel building structures. And there is reason to believe that MAP would work superbly in a coastal maritime environment—bridges, for example.'

Increasingly effective over time

The corrosion-protective effect also increases over time. This appears to be due to the formation of a composite film by MAP and corrosion products. At best, this spontaneously formed film has resulted in a reduction of as much as 99% in the corrosion rate.

The most effective forms of corrosion protection today are active ones that might be termed 'self-repairing' or 'self-healing'. If damage to the protective film arises, it can repair itself. This is how the chromate process works, for example. The MAP of the blue mussel has the same effect, and it can be used in both passive and active corrosion-protective films. Biopolymer Products has taken out patents on these discoveries.

Sticky proteins serve as glue: blue mussel

Blue mussels (*Mytilus edulis*)—bivalves that attach to rocks in wave-battered intertidal seashores—produce adhesives comparable in strength to human-made glues but without carcinogens such as formaldehyde and which can cure under water. A key feature of the blue mussel's unique adhesive chemistry are the presence of the amino acid 3,4-dihydroxyphenylalanine, with its reactive catechol functional group (two hydroxyl groups sticking out from a benzene ring) that forms strong bonds with catechols on adjacent molecules and with metal atoms present in the surface of most natural solid substrates. Another key feature is the ability of catechol chains to overcome a solid surface's otherwise strong preference for water molecules (which is why conventional adhesives fail on wet surfaces). New mussel-inspired adhesives, which have wide-ranging applications from surgical to wood composites, currently use soy as an inexpensive, accessible feedstock, and work by blocking certain amino acids in soy proteins that are not present in mussel proteins, such as glutamic acid, so that the resulting compound bears a closer resemblance to that of mussel proteins.

Biosciences: Kollodis

Mussel adhesive (MAP) protein was commercialized at first by a leading company known as Kollodis BioSciences. This company also commercialized some related products like MAP-based smart materials using MAPTrix. a proprietary platform. The development of Klidose with these new bimimeticmaterials and itssister products, these bioproducts got widespread popularity and demands all over the world. Klidose Bioscience now supplies a wide variety of products like Mussel Adhesive Protein (MAP) as bioadhesive, standalone adhesive, kit for ready to use, adhesive and adhesive variations specially needed by tissue culture technique, tissue engineering and related works, the MAPTrix extracellular matrix type of products. The MAPTrix Extracellular Matrix type products used as coating agents with bioactive peptides, genetically incorporated, i.e. recognition peptides. These peptides mimic the extracellular matrix (ECM) activity proteins like collagen, laminin, fibrinectin, cadherin, vitrinectin and heparin. This type of biologically active peptides has properties like cell attachment, growth and spreading. Another very important property of this bioactive peptide is its compatibility with living cells, hence immunological ejection reaction is low or absent. The company provides these bioactive peptides in a solution form in sealed vials, so it is easy to transport to distant places. It also supply recombinant mussel adhesive without bioactive peptide attached. Recently this company also initiated to supply HyGel— hydrogel—products useful for 3D cell culture and other similar applications. GF line of products—small peptide mimics of natural growth factors incorporated into a mussel adhesive protein that shows comparable biological activity to the naturally occurring growth factors. Our MAPTrix products are ready-to-use aqueous coating formulations that are biocompatible and free of animal-components, E. coli—proteins, and toxic chemicals. Our products are quality manufactured and performance tested in accordance with ISO/USP guidelines

Chapter-7

Modern town planning: Eco-friendly? LAVASA?

Sustainability of the world is in extremely dangerous. Forests are denuding year by year, atmosphere become polluted unpredictably, greenhouse gas level reaching at the zenith, global warming is a reality, drinking water shortage is in exclamatory, plastic wastage is uncontrollable, endangered species numbers are increasing world over, mass extinction of species is a big question, flood and their after-math is obvious, in spite of all these the world population is constantly increasing and may reach 7 billion mark shortly. Considering all these aspects sustainability should be given priority in all kind of developments. While the entire organisms in the nature living in harmony with nature human takes short cut for every movement, the result is imbalance in the nature. This imbalance is expressed by nature through devastating flood, earth quack, volcanic eruption, tsunami, global warming, drastic change in climate and many more natural calamities. The sufferer in these dumb and deaf plays of human is the innocent, amazingly large varieties of our biodiversity. Still, time is not too late we should understand the natures away and learn from it as we go along. Town planning and construction of new cities is not apart from these. Development, either gradual or abrupt must follow the natures laws, then only we can enjoy and being enjoyable for the coming generations of our kinds and millions of organisms that make our biodiversity.

Sustainable development concept should be the part and parcel of thinking in any kind of development. City also can be very sustainable places to live and act in harmony concerned with nature and natural process instead of defending it. Most of the developments in cities are not given much priority for this concept. An estimation of U.S council of green building reported that buildings are responsible for 70% of all electric consumption and 39% of CO_2 pollution, 40% energy consumption, 13% water consumption and 15 % GDP per year, making green building an important source of economic and environmental opportunity. Still the blooming of skyscrapers that use conventional energy is very negligible there. We should think, why do we are reluctant to construct building with this conventional energy? In this contest we must think about the biomimicry, innovation inspired by nature for sustainable development. Each and every construction must apply biomimicry principles so that we can reduce the current consumption to the ground level and the building automatically become sustainable. City planning and development also include biomimetic principles to make urban landscape to become a real sustainable place. This will pave the way for a pollution free development in the city. Naturally a question arise how we construct building according to the biomimetic principles. Hence, we should popularize the concept of biomimicry and biomimetic principles in a big way.

Biomimicry in Buildings

Green building or green construction or sustainable building is a new trend of practice of creating structures and using process that are environmentally responsible and resource efficient throughout the life of the building. The common objectives of the green building are:

1. Use water and other resources efficiently.
2. Take care of inhabitants' health and increase the productivity of the employees.
3. Pollution minimization and protect environment from its degradation.

Indian Green Building Council (IGBC) Green Homes is the first rating programmed developed in India, exclusively for the residential sector. It is a part of CII-Godrej Green Business Centre, which promote green building movement in India. The different members of the council involves government & nodal agencies, all stakeholders of construction industry comprising of corporate, product manufacturers, architects, institutions, etc. (Source: www.igbc.in). If green building is possible why not green city? Biomimcry is the first phase for the development of biomimetic shows should be encompassed. The eastgate center is an excellent example for this type of buildings. The building was constructed by inspiration from termite mounds. Termite maintains the internal temperature at 87 degree Fahrenheit by frequently closing and opening the cooling and heating vent. This type of ventilation system is found in Eastgate center, the largest office and shopping complex in Zimbabwe's, in which the outside air is frequently drawn in to cool and heat the building. The dead is air is exhausted through a outlet in the ceiling, hence the interior always remain cool. The building has no air conditioner and so save 10% energy. Similar to the eastgate National Museum in Washington, DC also have the same cooling system, which was built in 1880. In this way if we built a new city the energy and water saving must be unpredictable. More over the inhabitants are living in a natural place and thus prone to disease is minimal and protect the nature sustainable development; the ultimate goal of all the development is possible. As per my view if you keep aside all the political, and other commercial motto behind the LAVASA, the biomimicry principle applied in it is not full acceptable. We should observe the biomicry role in planning before begins its work, planned city.

Biomimicry-in-Planning

A city which mimics a well balanced ecosystem is always welcomed in the present era of pollution laden air. If a city constructed with recycling and reprocessing of all of its waste, it definitely well and good because it does not cause pollution of land, water and air and, i.e. the concept of sustainable development. LAVASA should concentrate on this side more than anything. As the trees and animals are the parts of nature human also the part of nature, hence the buildings and cities. Everything once is the part of the earth is to be realized everybody, and then only we can understand the great potential of the sustainable, biomimetic city. We should be consulted such an architectural developers city that should inspired and promote sustainable development. These architectural consultants look and understand the ecological aspects of the city's area and then only design how it will establish. Understanding the city ecology means Understanding the ecology of the city area means to know the details of the ecological factors like, how much rainfall should absorb by the ground in the city area and how much carbon should be created in this area etc. Just opposing on the ground of environment, development will sustain. We must think about the various possibilities to preserve our nature before the beginning of any development that directly affect the nature's biodiversity and other aspects. LAVASA is one of the cities that think a lot about this type of sustainability of the nature before its construction begin.

By considering this biomimcry background under sustainable development planning LAVASA may be one of the excellent examples in the world for ecofriendly-sustainable development planning for a new city. Whatever the motto behind the construction of the LAVASA, it is observed that, unknowingly due to much legal bondage the city forced to construct under strict obedience of laws of nature. But how much priority is given to the reprocessing of the various kind of waste that directly or indirectly disturbs the nature is still in debate. The building construction should be mimic nature's way as we seen in Eastgate Centre in Harare, Zimbabwe. Thanks to Indian laws and judiciary, an ideal one for any nation to follow.

Sustainable development and sustainability.

Sustainable development and sustainability influence today's urban planners. Some planners argue that modern lifestyles use too many natural resources, polluting or destroying ecosystem, increasing social inequality, creating urban heat island, and causing climate change. Many urban planners, therefore, advocate sustainable cities (Wheeler, 1998). Wheeler (1998) lists a 'sustainable' city's features: compact, efficient land use; less automobile use, yet better access; efficient resource use; less pollution and waste; the restoration of natural systems; good housing and living environments; a healthy social ecology; a sustainable economy; community participation and involvement; and preservation of local culture and wisdom. LAVASA should assess on basis of this proposal. No political interference and no compromise of any kind should be curtailed time to time to achieve such a developmental process.

Let us examine the site of LAVASA before and after its construction begins.

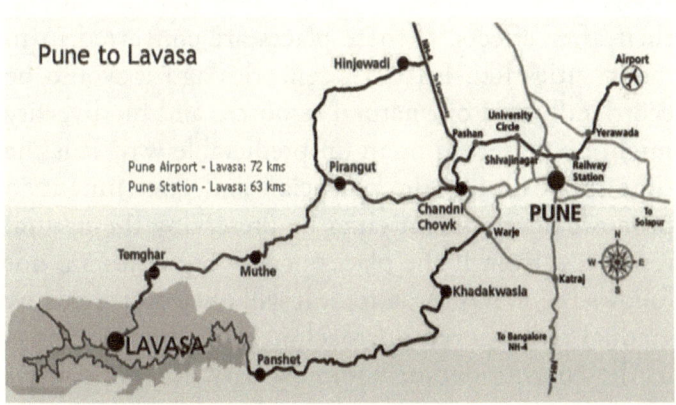

By examining these picturesque we may have a feeling that the project is excellent. Really it is excellent; the growing population in India needs an urgent awareness and initiation to lead a world class life style without harm the nature. Janine Benyus, world-renowned biologist, innovation consultant and author of six books including *Biomimicry: Innovation Inspired by Nature,* says "Today, we need corporate and business leaders to choose the path less trodden. We need new ideas and we need to revolutionize the way we live, create and exist. Lavasa is a brilliant attempt towards creating a human dwelling to emulate nature's ideas. We need many more Lavasas in the world in order to ensure we last longer on planet earth" (Workshop, Mumbai, March 9th 2010). If the development of the city LAVASA obeys the rules and regulation of the nature the project is affordable and adequate. The vast majority of lands near Pune or Mumbai or any so called well developed city in India or in the world are once a beautiful landscape and natures abode. These natural resources in these areas are destructed by construction of concrete buildings, skyscrapers, traffics and human over population and their after effects. If these places are converted in to major cities like LAVASA centuries ago it would be ecofriendly and our natural resources and biodiversity might be preserved in an un-predictable way. It is the time for re-thinks the politician and government to promote development cities by preserving the natural resources. Even if the places nearby big cities are not follows the LAVASA pattern, it will once destructed by gradual and uneven encroachment of human beings in the coming decades unknowingly. In this contest as per my view the pattern and policies developed by LAVASA is acceptable partially, but the other side should not be encouraged. While encouraging this type of sustainable development a strict over look and strong adherence of the laws of both government and nature should be follow. A lot of examples of such movements are available world over. The meaning of sustainable urban development explained in different ways by different people, but what actually it means? *Brundtland Commission* cited the definition as "development that meets the needs of the present without compromising the ability of future generations to meet their own needs." (Rees, William E. and Roseland, Mark. 1991. Sustainable Communities: Planning for the 21st Century. Plan Canada. 31: 3. 15.). A conference was held at Berlin, July 2000 known as URBAN21 Conference, this conference given a different definition for the sustainable development as "Improving the quality of life in a city, including ecological, cultural, political, institutional, social and economic components without leaving a burden on the future generations. A burden is the result of a reduced natural capital and an excessive local debt. Our aim is that the flow principle that is based on equilibrium of material and energy and also financial input/output plays a crucial role in all future decisions upon the development of urban areas". But there are many more definitions stem up in the same conference for various purposes of sustainable development.

One of the important definitions to be mention is "Sustainable community development is the ability to make development choices which respect the relationship between the three "E's"-Economy, Ecology, and Equity:

E-Economic: It promulgated that activity should serve the common good, be self-renewing, and build local assets and self-reliance.

E-Ecology: Human apart of ecosystem has responsibility to harm the natural system least and save something to the future.

E-Equity: It promulgated that the opportunity for full participation in all activities, benefits, and decision-making of a society.

All these definitions has it own value, but the essence of the definitions is the one that is keep the natural resources and biodiversity for the future while extracting for the present existence.

An overlook on LAVASA

Near Pune, the city LAVASA was erected by private agencies. The total area covers about 25,000 acres (100 km²) or 8,000 acres (32 km²). The project being developed by HCC, but remain as incomplete city due to various controversies including procurement of land, harm to the environment, and loans acquired through political corruption. In 2010, Indian Environment and Forest Ministry requested to stop all the works going on there. The ministry claims that it violate environmental laws prevailed in India. LAVASA is the first artificially built hill station in India since independence. This city is being constructed by a unit of Ajit Gulabchand's. Hindustan Construction Company better known as Lavasa Corporation. The area located near Pune in the Westren Ghat, on the banks of the Baji Pasalkar Reservoir behind the Varsagoan Dam in the Mose valley.

Lavasa: A Corporation

Lavasa located in the picturesque landscape of the Sahayadri Mountains. From Mumbai, it requires three hour drive to LAVASA and 1 hour from Pune. It is about 1/5th size of Mumbai. Internationally renowned design consultant HOK, USA is designed the LAVASA city plane for about 18,000 acres. HOK is a recipient of many international awards in this field. The plane is designed in such a way that all amenities for a normal life should be available in a walk able distance. Really, it is an awe inspiring development spanning over 23,014 acres of picturesque and lush landscape. The city is located in front of picturesque lakefront and extended over seven magnificent hills. Lavasa is the largest urban infrastructure project in India because it provides good economic benefit in this region. It is a unique architectural design in which a mega city is standing among the greenery without hurting the natural beauty, and reforestation and slop greening is an additional advantage with priority in the project. LAVASA is an example for industrial development under natural inhabitant and ecosystem. The factories constructing in this area has to follow strict norms that even not causing a single ppm pollution particles in the vicinity. It provide 365 day economy by providing job opportunities like R&D and training centers, IT and biotech industry, KPOs and those related to art, fashion and animation. Lavasa has many firsts to its credit—technology leadership; the first Indian city developed using Geographical Information System (GIS), use of Biomimicry as a science in town planning and use of innovative techniques like hydro seeding in environment management.

Environmental initiatives at LAVASA

1. Watershed Management: over 200 acres
2. Mass Plantation: over 6 lakh indigenous plants
3. Mass seeding using local seeds: over 500 acres including hydro seeding
4. Plantation of local shrubs and stumps: over 6 lakh
5. Mass fertilization: over 40 metric tons to enhance soil quality
6. Soil Bioengineering: slope protection measures using eco-friendly material such as coir, soil and bamboo to create living slopes
7. Mass plantation effort certified under organic practices
8. Regular monitoring of environment parameters over and above the statutory stipulations.

If this entire proposed target is in really meant what it means, a sustainable development should be achieved. The remaining part is the construction of buildings. All these planning are an amazing example of a sustainable city construction plan. In this way in LAVASA also the building should be self-sustained one, means each and every building of any kind must have rain water harvesting facility, water recycling unit, waste management system, solar panel for the whole building energy consumption of all kinds. The public utilities like street light and other energy consuming system must be operated through solar energy. The building should be constructed as seen in Eastgate Centre, so that we can avoid artificial air cooling machinery and consequently energy consumption at ground level. The vehicles should be used minimum so that air pollution can be managed effectively. The city authorities should monitor pollution level of any kind time to time, if any anomaly observed it should be promptly corrected. The water table level must be checked time to time otherwise it will affect the water supply and the water resources will decline unpredictably. The hill top must be maintained its height while construction work is progressing, otherwise the water table level will decline; the water reservoir will dry up, bore well need to bore greater depth to dig up water, valleys greenery will wilt away due to the scarcity of water. This means we should predict the ecological backlash to be happening decades later for the development of new cities like LAVASA. Biomimcry experts will assists in this contest greatly. In short the LAVASA should be a self-sustained one to attain the goal of biomimetic city. From the progress of the work it is observed that the movement initiated by LAVASA authorities in the construction of new city is in right direction. Let us hope that LAVASA will be an amazing example of biomimetic city in the world. Restriction of the use of material must be a policy from the part of government to reduce the waste in the biomimetic city. Through the Toxics Release Inventory (TRI), one can know at a glance what kinds of chemicals are being used, and how much of each chemical is being released into the environment. This is a policy that induces corporations to voluntarily reduce their discharge by having each corporation report the types and amounts of chemicals discharged into the environment to the Ministry of Environment, which then shares the report data with the government, corporations, and the people. This policy has had a hugely positive result, with many corporations assessing the types and amounts of chemicals discharged to the environment through internal processes, and attempting to reduce their discharge amounts through various means. TRI is a system that has already been executed in many other countries including the US, Japan and the EU. India must execute the TRI system, especially in the biomimetic city. In the TRI, the discharge information on various chemicals can be verified. For example, what kinds of chemicals were discharged, and in what quantity? What types and quantities of chemicals were discharged in a certain industrial area? What types and quantities of chemicals did certain types of businesses discharge? Citizens are encouraged to take an interest in the information disclosed through the Toxics Release Inventory, and to become monitors that encourage corporations to voluntarily reduce their toxic emissions. The interest and actions of citizens, however small, can have an enormous influence in decreasing the amount of toxic discharge and encouraging the safe management of chemicals. The toxics Release Inventory is a system that is formulated by the people themselves, and thus requires the active participation of citizens. Corporations also must continuously communicate with interest groups, such as residents and citizens groups, as well as the press, regarding the types of toxics that are being released and the question of what is needed to reduce the discharge amount, and should also prepare a risk communication system that is ready in the event of any accidental release during the production process. One caution when referring to the TRI is that the release amount is computed according to the amount of toxins release into the environment, and does not indicate direct exposure or risk level for humans or the ecosystem. To assess the exposure probability and risk resulting from the release of toxins into the environment, a variety of information other than the release inventory is required. Implementation of "the Industrial Waste Reduction System" will reduce the volume of wastes generated or disposed of, or its harmfulness by decreasing waste or promoting recycling in the production process. Food waste is one of the great problems in cities. A bio-mimicking city should take care to reduce the waste generated through food wastes or it should be harmlessly recycled. As a part of efforts to promote food waste-to-energy policy, the government required developers of building lots and tourist spots to install food waste-to-energy facilities by revising the Enforcement Decree of the Promotion of Installation of Waste Disposal Facilities and Assistance. Poorly managed waste management systems in cities do not only cause serious environmental pollution, but also make it hard for domestic environmental establishments to make inroads into overseas environmental markets. In this regard I propose to follow Korea, Korea aims at sharing model cases of green growth through the transfer of Korea's sophisticated environmental policy & technology to developing countries and making profits via receiving construction orders. (Ministry of environment, Korea: http://eng.me.go.kr/main.do). Medical wastes is another great waste category we face in the city. These wastes must be treated properly to maintain bio-mimic city. Medical wastes shall be contained in exclusive containers. Of hazardous medical wastes, isolation medical waste, tissue distribution waste and injurious waste, as well as all liquid waste shall be kept in box-type exclusive containers that are made of synthetic resins, and the container in which liquid waste is kept shall have a lock so that the cover cannot be opened. Other wastes can be kept in containers that are made of corrugated cardboard. Medical wastes shall be disposed of by a certified medical wastes disposer. In the event that the institution that produces the medical wastes wants to dispose of them by itself, a facility for the sterilization and pulverization of medical wastes can be installed in the institution. The biomimcking city must follow the waste to energy policy. The waste to energy policy is an effective method to respond to climate change arising from the global warming effect of Methane, which has a heat-trapping effect in the atmosphere that is 21 times stronger than that of Carbon Dioxide, because it replaces fossil fuels and reduces the generation of Methane gas. Recently, countries around the globe are striving to reduce greenhouse effects by using Refuse-derived fuel (RDF) made from combustible solid wastes to produce energy. In particular, the EU has set the goal of reducing 320million tons of CO_2 through the waste to energy program by 2010, and has implemented the measure. In order to more actively implement the waste to energy policy, the city need to expand manufacturing RDF using combustible solid wastes and exclusive power generation, electricity generation and purification projects using bio-gasification of organic waste, like advanced countries do. Cities have large potential for waste energy generation using, for example, combustible & organic waste, house hold resources and garbage. Advanced countries such as Germany and Japan have created independent bio-energy towns utilizing sewage sludge, food waste, livestock manual and forest, agricultural by-product (http://eng.me.go.kr). In order achieve a better biomimcking city LAVASA should follow this kind of waste-energy converting system. National Solid Waste Association of India (NSWAI), a leading organization, which is non-profit and help in the management of solid waste, biomedical waste and other sort of waste possibly produced in the LAVSA. NSWAI is a member of ISWA—International Solid Waste Association, Copenhagen, Denmark. This international organization provides council for transcontinental and national level advice for management of different kind of wastes. Functional biomimcking or self-sustained city is reflected from recycling of each and every kind of materials used by the inhabitants of the city. Waste material can be made to useful one by recycling process. Collection of different kinds of waste like bottles, cane, used toys, and other plastic and non-plastic material is the first step in the recycling process, it also provide small scale business to generate income for the poor sections. Another benefit of recycling, it reduce land filling and incineration, pollution and save energy. It also reduce greenhouse gases, which cause global warming, and moreover it reduce the aggressive use natural resources like timber, water, and minerals, finally sustainable development is the result of recycling waste materials. LAVASA will concentrate in a big way to this kind of recycling as the authorities' claims. The preservation of natural ecosystem hand in hand with the development of the LAVASA city is an ideal model development of modern city. If the biodiversity is not harmed and natural wealth is not denude then such kind of development is acceptable. LAVASA is one of such kind of city in the world. If city is purely a conglomeration of buildings and overpopulation burdened with millions of vehicles of varied nature then air pollution will be an increasing menace and cannot be controlled any way. This is the trend in big Indian cities. In Indian cities like Ahmadabad, Varanasi, Chennai, Pune, and Kolkata the PM10 levels have reduced in 2007 compared to 2002 levels. However in the cities like Mumbai, Faridabad, Luck now, Bangalore and Delhi the PM10 (Particulate matter) annual average levels have increased in 2007 over 2002 (Center of science and environment, http://www.cseindia.org). The nitrogen dioxide levels in the cities like Sholapur, Ahmadabad, Pune and Kolkata has reduced (CSE). According to CPCB, although various interventions have taken place to mitigate ambient NO_2 levels but at the same time number of vehicles has increased exponentially. The vehicles are one of the major sources of NO_2. Measures taken to mitigate ambient NO_2 levels are introduction of improved vehicular technology in the form of Bharat Stage-III vehicles, banning of old vehicles in some cities, improved traffic management etc. In such situation if a city like LAVASA having a lot of natural vegetation's will reduce the air pollution including PM naturally without any extra cost of energy and wealth. Therefore development of biomimcking city should be encouraged and is the necessity of the present age. A living example for the role of natural vegetation on the reduction of air pollution is the south Indian cities like Thiruvantapuram, Cochin and Mysore where the PM10 levels are gradually reducing during 2000-2007 like Simla, Parwanoo and Gajraula like hill stations. also have low PM10 levels (CSE, http://www.cseindia.org). In this respect if the trend of LAVASA preserving the natural habitat and biodiversity is continuing and be a part of the city planning policy, it will emerge as the best biomicking city. Most of the new cities developed in the world over are built in remote areas where human inhabitation is very poor but biodiversity is immense. For example in Singapore the Queenstown (1952-1973) built by public housing authority of Singapore, this organization construct about 11,000 public houses are built over 22 towns in Singapore. Each and every town built by this organization is self sustainable. Similarly many cities like Tsuen Wan and Kwun Tong (Honkong), Helsinki (Finland), Dunaujvaros, Tiszaujvaros, Kazincbarcika (Hungary) are built in small villages or islands. Building new cities definitely cause some instant bad effect on the environment, but if we planned well to protect the biodiversity and natural resources, and use the concept of sustainable development then the new city will become a facsimile of its original status. We cannot forbid the development of new cities because it is the need of the growing population. The better way is "prevention is better than cure", yes curtail the population growth to the maximum then all the city becomes once a barren place. This impossible thing makes the development of possible new cities. LAVASA is not an exemption in this regard. The concept is originated from the need of the people; the difference is that it is exploited by somebody. Hence brewing the soup in somebody's bowls and others taste the smell only even though has the eagerness to have in our own bowl. The newly granted one, "Environment Minister Mr. Jairam Ramesh on Monday sanctioned solid approval to Orissa, which divert 1,253 hectares of forest for Posco's steel project . . . ." Shows that LAVASA might be correct (The Hindu: Business Line, May 2nd 2011). It further says that, "POSCO would also bear the cost of regeneration of an equivalent amount of open, degraded land in a district to be determined and indicated by the state Government", LAVASA may follow the same criteria and fulfill the requirement of the government by time bounded basis. This attitude will protect new city and regenerate an equal land of forest also

CHAPTER-8

Some case studies in biomimcry

Scorpions inspire scientists in making tougher surfaces for machinery

Yellow fantail scorpion gave us inspiration, it protect itself against scratches from desert sandstorms by using a bionic shield. By getting inspiration from this scientists have developed technology to save the parts which are moving in machinery from damage. Zhiwu Han, Junqiu Zhang, Wen Li and colleagues described this as "solid particle erosion" is always and main reasons for damage of material or failure equipment. It may results in multi millllion dollars of damage every year to rocket motor nozzles, helicopter rotors, pipes, turbine blades and other parts of mechanical. Actually the damage is due to the abrasion of particles of grit, dirt and other tough material in the water, air, or other fluids hit the surfaces of the target parts. One way to remove the particles is to use filters but it needs to be replaced or make clean, but tougher, erosion-resistant materials will cost more to make and develop. Han and Li's group make an effort to develop better erosion-resistant surfaces by copying the secrets of the scorpion—yellow fantail for the first time. By the process of natural selection scorpion is survived by the abrasive power of rough sandstorms. They really studied the decoration on the back of the scorpion i.e.

bumps and grooves, 3-D laser device scanning of the species and manipulating a computer based program that mimics the flow of sand-laden air on the back the scorpions. They also used computer simulations model to develop real surface pattern to verify which patterns perform best. Simple erosion wind tunnel experiment also designed for groove surface bionic samples with different pressure conditions. These scientists' discovery leads to produce stele with better erosion resistant surface. Thanks god for this miniature creature to save us from erosion of stele from moisture and other humid atmosphere.

Snakes improve search-and-rescue robots

Scientists face very difficult to produce and design all-terrain robot for various purpose like search-and-rescue missions. The main requirement is the flexibility of the machine, it is essential to move over harsh and uneven surfaces, but at the same time it should be small enough to operate in small restricted spaces. The other requirement is it must be able to climb a slop of different angles, inclines. Available robots also can do the same huge amount of energy and always cause overheating. Researchers from Georgia Tech recently have prepared a new machine by copying the mode of movement and locomotion of a particular type of type of flexible, efficient animal. For example snakes are able to creep long distance without causing much friction, energy and heating the surface by using the scales adorned on the surface. The researchers from the same institute studied by videotaping movements of about 20 varied species at Zoo Atlanta. The outcome of their study is a robot named Scalybot 2. This mimics the rectilinear movement of reptiles-snakes. He presented the robot at the Society for Integrative & Comparative Biology (SICB) in Charleston, annual meeting. It is interesting that during the movement of snakes it did not bend its body laterally. It is observed that during its locomotion snakes lift its ventrals and pull themselves by muscular dwindling waves from head to tail. This type of movement is very effective and useful while creeping within the crevices. This secret copied in Scalybot 2 so that it changes the angle of its scales when it face or encounter uneven slopes and terrains. This is very profitable because it cannot generate friction or heat. Further if it is connected with remote to shift forward and backward and sideways it is very helpful to control without going to the dangerous terrains and slopes. Snakes are generally very maligned and dangerous creature but the work of Georgia Tech researcher made it friendly to the technical world by providing the secret of new flexible, frictionless and non-overheating robots" Scalybot 2".

Leaping lizards and dinosaurs inspire robot design

Biologist and engineers from University of California, Berkeley, studied and revealed the secret of lizards leap successfully even when they accidently slip and stumble. They found that when they move swinging the tail upward. This is to protect them during a forward pitch by send them head-over-heels into an object or tree. This stimulated many scientisms to add a tail to a robotic car and named it as Tailbot. Both Robots and lizards have to make a particular angle of their tail, before falling, just right to counteract the effect of the stumble. By the same mechanism of tail angle control a robots can make a leap and remain upright. Inspiration from lizard may lead to design more accurate, valuable and user friendly robots in the future. It may also used to detect dangerous radioactive, biological or nuclear hazards. Here we can recall the movie Jurassic park; in this movie the leaping movement of lizards followed the same patter. Dinosaur is more efficient in controlling the tail movement due to its heavy body size and, muscle may act effectively in this movement. The discoverer send the article to Nature for publication. They have planned to present the paper in at the annual meeting of the Society for Integrative and Comparative Biology in Charleston, South Carolina.

From gecko toe hairs to tails

Gecko's locomotion on varied surface is a matter of amazing for many. A scientist Full did a lot of research in this animal to find out the secret of gecko's walk on the undersurface of roof without slipping down. Full was actively in research for the last 20 years and reveled finally how hairs on gecko's toe allow the animal to climb on smooth and vertical surface and recently researcher turns to how their tails help to prevent falling when their feet fails to grip and remain in the mid-air. The tail movement during the locomotion of gecko is inspired many scientist to design well balanced robot when the robot move through uneven and stony rumbling surface during rescue operations. The recent researcher experimentally tested the secret biped theropod, bird like ancestors lived as contemporaries of dinosaurs. The bird like dinosaurs used their tails to as a balancing organ while running or dodging obstacles and predators. Full used high speed videography and motion capture to study the leaping and jumping of red-headed African Agama lizard managed leaps from specially prepared platform with varied degree of traction, from very slippery to gripped sand papers. These scientist provoked the lizard to run and jump over obstacles and then to climb over a vertical surface to reach the shelter on top. They noticed that when the surface become more slippery they slipped and causing their body to spin to particular angle and loss control. The researcher observed how the lizard used its tail to counter balance its body during this spinning of body and created a mathematical model and tailbot to study more about these animal's skill. A sensor was attached to the robot to sense the spin and send the message to the tail of tailbot and the tailbot automatically stabilize the body in mid air. Thus gecko inspired us to design a better robot, thanks to the gecko for his brilliant natural gift given by the natural selection mechanism.

Insect cyborgs may become first responders

It is a common practice to test hazardous chemicals by using non-human animals or invertebrates before reaching human use. Engineers from University of Michigan College of Engineering used insects experimentally to monitor hazardous moment before reaching in humans. Students, professors and some researchers are on the way to harvest energy from insects and make the use of miniature cybrogs to further level.

The way these peoples did is to locate a tiny backpacks contain microphones, potentially power camera and other sensors and communication machines. These insects are then left to dangerous environment where man cannot dare to go. Here actually we harvest the biological energy stored in the insect's body either in the form of heat or movement. The machine converts kinetic energy of the insect's wing movement into electrical energy and increase the battery life. This battery then can be used for operating the sensor put on backpack of the insect to collect and send important information regarding the dangerous environment where man cannot go. A l piezoelectric generator can be used to increase the efficiency of the compliant one in limited place. This type of technology can be used to fabricate process to machine high aspect ratio devises to huge piezoelectric substrates with few dames by using femtosecond laser

Supercomputer seeks way to mimic mollusk shell

Warwick's new super computer is used recently to examine the properties of the tiny mollusc shell endowed by natural selection. We know that the mollusc shell is fabricated of only one kind of mineral i.e. calcium carbonate. But the secret lies in the fact that this mineral along with some enzymes and proteins give it, such an amazing properties, like extraordinary strength with extraordinary light weight. By copying this property scientists are hoping to guide to make materials which mimic natural properties in a synthetic format. It definitely modernizes the building materials in the coming years and may improve synthetic bone substitutes for orthopedic operation, especially hip replacement surgery. In the present world of computer Warwick's computer remains an entity that we cannot compete with any other computer so far made. Millions of million operations in a fraction of second that need weeks or more will do by Warwick's computer within a fraction of minutes or second. An extra ordinary example of how nature inspired us to speed up our leap in the technical world. Mother Nature gives gifts in the form of secrets that we have to explore step by step. To explore these secret for long period we have to keep something for the future generation and hence sustainable development. By the discovery of computer and super computer we are only in the miniature niche of the nature where we have to explore many, many things hidden in the lap of the Mother Nature. We salute to the great ability of nature to create such a materials on the surface molluscan shell, that also under low temperature and pollution free chemicals that we cannot design in the laboratory without high temperature and millions of dollars and more over high pollution is amazing.

Bats, dolphins, and mole rats inspire advances in ultrasound technology

Bats, dolphins, and mole rats, inspired us many new ideas. Recently scientists over the world are searching the secret of how animals measure the returning signals. It is nothing but a superior—supra natural ability to data processing. The echolocation ability of animals in a fraction of a second with high precision and high resolution is amazing. For example, A dolphin can see a tennis ball from approximately 260 feet away." This is nothing but the ability of dolphin and other such animals having the power of echolocation, to compute and process millions of tiny images into a single one in a fraction of second. The high computing ability of a supra computer doing the same thing and hence we thanks to the great creator of such animal and the secret that we can copy for our welfare.

Detecting "shape" from sound

"Pings" are ultra sonic sound emitted by biosensor animals in the environment. These animals detect (see) the object from the shape of the returning waves or echoes. This ability helps them to navigate or hunt their prey. It is a fact that neurons in animal's brain are capable of full scale analyzing the surroundings and convert it into a three dimensional images within tens of milliseconds, that also with minimum energy consumption. We cannot design such an accurate, precise picture even by using our computer or super computer. A bat can differentiate a fly either in motion of static with his echolocation power that is not, sees a bat can determine which fruit is heavier and which one is lighter by its echolocation device by just observing the fruits movement in wind. Researcher studying the echolocation ability by manipulating the returning waves by obstructing with some electromagnetic waves. This type of research may lead us to design better device to help are blind and deaf.

Borrowing from brightly-colored birds: Physicists develop lasers inspired by nature

The feather of birds is amazingly bright coloured and is matter of research for both engineering technology and biologist. The colour is produced by two types of nano scale structure on the feather of birds. Researchers hopping that this secret of birds feather colour can be used to produce new types of lasers-ones that can assemble themselves by natural processes. In some birds, these structures produce iridescence, because colors change with the angle of view-like the soap bubble. In other birds, the colour produced by the nanostructure is steady and unchanging. The mechanism which causing these colour changes is fascinated by many scientists; it may be due to the random jumbling of proteins. But when researchers zoomed in on small sections of the protein at a time, quasi-ordered patterns began to emerge. The scientists found that it is this short-range order that scatters light preferentially at specific frequencies to produce the distinctive hues of a bluebird's wings. Based on these findings researcher from various universities are now produce various laser equipments which cause color variation when focusing on the specially prepared nano structure, mimicking the bird feather, surface on different angles. By this technique different sign boards can be prepared and may be use for traffic signaling system for various warning signals.

What makes these short-range-ordered, bio-inspired structures different from traditional lasers is that, in principle, they can self-assemble, through natural processes similar to the formation of gas bubbles in a liquid. This means that engineers would not have to worry about the nanofabrication of the large-scale structure of the materials they design, resulting in cheaper, faster, and easier production of lasers and light-emitting devices.

One potential application for this work includes more efficient solar cells that can trap photons before converting them into electrons. The technology could also yield long-lasting paint, which could find uses in processes such as cosmetics and textiles.

Auto-pilots need a birds-eye view

Robotics and auto-pilots are the result of new research birds can fly and its ability to fly quickly and accurately through dense forests. Scientists created artificial forest and allowed birds to fly in the forest by attaching camera at its head and captured images as bird's eye view. The camera give images of birds fly as well as images of birds eye. Previously pigeon was used to navigate through different drastic and difficult environmental condition. The pigeon methods can be used as a model for auto-pilot technology. For this purpose bird with >300 degree panoramic vision are commonly used because it allow them to see obstacles on either side. A small rapid movement of head called "head saccade" which can be used to stabilize their vision and change rapidly between views. This finding was presented at the Society for Experimental Biology annual conference in Glasgow, 2011. The other skills of the birds like moving straight route is also can be used for the auto-pilot mechanism. This ability of birds can be used efficiently flying through thick forest without hitting to the branches and other obstacles, with least turns and expenditure of energy. Another interesting facts observed about birds is its ability to remember the way they entered the forest and exit through the same route without any confusion. If we copy this mastermind of birds in a robot we can reach the interior part of the forest and even in the deeper part of ocean by simple modification of the technology. Thanks to the amazing ability of pigeon and other birds to embodied this ability to navigate forest interior.

Is the hornet our key to renewable energy?

Plants ability to convert solar energy to chemical energy is the base for the existence of life on earth. This ability of the plants is due to its chloroplast and tiny structure grana and thylkoid membranes. It is now discovered that Oriental hornet can convert solar energy into chemical energy by using its yellow and brown parts of its body. Thanks to the Tel Aviv University team for these findings. If this become a reality we can copy the same principle in other animals we can harvest solar energy in a massive manner.

Discovering a new system for renewable energy?

Previously, entomologists noted that Oriental wasps, unlike other wasps and bees, are active in the afternoon rather than the morning when the sun is just rising. They also noticed that the hornet digs more intensely as the sun's intensity increases.

Taking this information to the lab, the Tel Aviv University team studied weather conditions like temperature, humidity and solar radiation to determine if and how these factors also affected the hornet's behavior, but found that UVB radiation alone dictated the change. In the course of their research, the Tel Aviv University team also found that the yellow and brown stripes on the hornet abdomen enable a photo-voltaic effect: the brown and yellow stripes on the hornet abdomen can absorb solar radiation, and the yellow pigment transforms that into electric power.

The team determined that the brown shell of the hornet was made from grooves that split light into diverging beams. The yellow stripe on the abdomen is made from pinhole depressions, and contains a pigment called xanthopterin. Together, the light diverging grooves, pinhole depressions and xanthopterin change light into electrical energy. The shell traps the light and the pigment does the conversion.

A biological heat pump

Number of energy processes unique to the insect was found by many researchers. Like refrigerators and air conditioners, the hornet has a well-developed heat pump system in its body which keeps it cooler than the outside temperature while it forages in the sun.

If we reproduce this secret of hornet it will be a renewable source of energy. The research also discovered that hornets use finely honed acoustic signals to guide them so they can build their combs with extraordinary precision in total darkness.

Researchers gain focus on a bug with bifocals

Bug with bifocals was reported by researchers of University of Cincinnati. The researcher explained that using two retinas and two distinct focal planes that are substantially separated. These bifocals can use the larvae more efficiently. Compared with the glasses that humans wear, to switch their vision from up-close to distance— the better to see and catch their prey, with their favorite food being mosquito larvae. The research also described that each eyes can be used separately and focused separate images on retina and will function as separate eye in one eye. This research will hold implications in human and increase the possibility of new research in biomedical engineering. This discovery also helps for any imaging technology. The larvae of the sunburst diving beetle larvae have bifocal lens. It was studied in creeks and streams around Arizona and the western United States. Sunburst diving beetle classified as a holometabolous insect like the caterpillar/moth or the maggot/fly. The larvae lose the sophisticated lenses when they become an adult beetle.

Tough yet stiff deer antler is materials scientist's dream

People hunt deer for its decorative antler and getting money from international market. But the antler is more precious than its cost and decoration as proclaimed by some researchers in the field of biomimcry. They used this antler as fighting weapons during dueling. Antlers appear to be dry but no one knows really it is dry or look as if they are dry. It is interesting to find out whether the antler is dry or wet and how it affect the mechanical properties of antler. It is also essential to compare the dryness of a bone before testing the dryness of the antler. The experimental procedure involves testing the dryness after acollecting the antler form stag after shedding its protective velvet for every week. It is observed by researcher that antler loss a colossal 8% of its weight. It will be 1% loss if it cut at another season of the year. Finally stabilized the weight loss and the antler's humidity remain in balance with that of the surrounding air. Thus we can conclude that the antler may dry when the stag begins dueling. The amazing result obtained by researchers in the field prove that antlers strength and flexibility many times greater than wet bones. Usually bones become brittle when it dries so that it cannot be an ideal material for weapons. Antler on the contrast is stronger and flexible and tougher and unbreakable than same piece of femur bone. It is observed that antler is 24 times tougher than femur and it could survive 6 times greater than the force that shatters the femur bone. So dry deer antlers are simultaneously tough, yet stiff making them perfectly suited to their role as a weapon. Thus the deer help to solve a problem that has puzzled engineers for many decades. To make anything that is both stiff and tough is very difficult. Thanks to the dueling of deer with antler.

Scientists are first to 'unlock' the mystery of creating cultured pearls from the queen conch

Culturing pearls from the queen conch (*Strombus gigas*) have been unsuccessful since last 25 years and even today. But now researchers from Florida University solved this intriguing problem by novel and proprietary seeding techniques. By this technique they successed in producing beaded (nucleated) and non-beaded cultured pearls from the queen conch. Scientist from the same university prepared about 200 cultured pearls using the techniques they developed, that also with less than two years. Before this experiment no high-quality queen conch pearl had been cultured. This experiment gifted a new technology to produce the pearls to the industry. This technique is comparable to the technique developed in Japan in 1920 for pear oyster. Gemological Institute of America (GIA) is involved in extensive research in pearl culturing by applying various examinations like chemical composition, spectroscopy, spectrometry and microscopic methods. Queen conch culture was impossible previously may be due to the fact that the shell is spiral in shape, this shape make it difficult to reach the gonads, which is the pearl forming region in pearl oyster that also without damaging the animal's life. The major advantage of this type technique is that it does not sacrifice the conch in the process. The 100 percent survival ability of the queen conch makes it very profitable as it makes generation of generation new conch with making any bad effect on pearl products. The survival of queen conch is very important because it is an threatened species in many part of the world.

The method involves adding concentric layer around the dent, this layering often produce desired flame structure, a characteristic feature of conch pearl. The pearl is now available in variety of colour and shape.

Secrets of insect flight revealed

The secret to produce and design a micro-aircraft that flies with maneuverability and energy efficiency of an insect is revealed recently by some researcher in the field of biomimcry. This technique was developed by decoding the aerodynamic secret of insect flight. The researcher used high-speed digital video cameras to record locusts in action in a wind tunnel and recording how the shape of a locust's wing changes in flight. The information collected was used to create a computer model which simulates the airflow and thrust generated by the complex flapping movement. This information can be important to the creation of miniature robot flyers for use in situations such as search and military, rescue, applications and inspecting environments which is very hazardous. Optimization of biological systems through evolutionary pressures for millions of years given has us many examples of performance that we cannot achieve artificially. The insect wing, decoration and twist, curve, ridges, wrinkled surface are far away as we can get from the streamlined wing of an aircraft Measurement of the wings in insect is little bit complicate because the wings are not uniform in shape and the flight is so heavy that we cannot measure it. One of the most common insect, locusts is always inspired by engineers because of its long distance flight with minimum usage of energy. The researcher studied the secret of various decorations on the insect wings by removing ridges, wrinkles, curves separately and studied the lifting and flight pattern. It is observed that by removing the ridges insect find difficulty in raising the body and so as groves and curves. This means that the ridges, curves and wrinkles perform their own duty specifically in different pattern of flight. If we mimic this secret in our aerodynamic machine we can do as insect with least effort and energy expenditure and is the need today due to shortage fuels and fuel crisis. Researchers and biomimcry specialists are now turn to simulate the insect wing patter and efficiency in human made aerodynamic machines, so that we can make easy, less expensive and more comfortable intercontinental flight.

Secrets of the sandcastle worm could yield a powerful medical adhesive

Sandcastle worm, a tiny creature, living in the sea has secret glue that works in water. Scientists have copied this natural glue to develop an a long-sought medical adhesive to repair bones damaged in car crashes, battlefield injuries and other accidents. This synthetic glue is based on complex coacervates. Mussel adhesives is one of the natural adhesive known as very early and it has been in use for various operation involving bone shattering during accidents. After this, mussel adhesive discovery, along gap 30 years are there without any modifications in this direction. Today, the Sandcastle worm adhesive is so very important to mention. The old method of bone fracture repair involves many non-biomaterials like nails, screw, taps, steel rods etc; all these will cause immunological rejection and complications. Hence biodegradable and biocompatible materials like mussel adhesive and recently Sandcastle worm glue catch attention of many scientific and non-scientific and commercial peoples alike. The glue that sandcastle worms (*Phragmatopoma californica*) secreted was duplicated by Stewart and colleagues while building their homes in intertidal surf by sticking together bits of sand and broken sea shells. The worm stick to the harsh surface under the water to protect themselves from current of water, this secret of remaining the glue insoluble in wet environments and was able to bond to wet objects is amazing. The study shows that it is non-toxic, and as stronger as super glue and twice stronger than natural glue available. The properly of this sandcastle worm glue i.e. insoluble in water, have good strength and resistant to many chemicals make it ideal for many places in medical field like teeth fixing and manipulation, bone fracture repair and many other such incidence.

What scientists know about jewel beetle shimmer?

Jewel beetles are well known for its glossy external skeleton that changes its colour when the angle of view changes. Today Jewel beetles are known for one which providing blueprint for materials that produce colour by reflecting and not by absorbing. Researcher from Georgia institute of technology in Atlanta discovered the secret of colour changing behavior of the Jewel Beetles. They claim that the cells present on the exoskeleton have light reflecting property and this reflecting property is reason for the colour change and not the light absorbing property of the pigments as in other animals e.g. chameleon. This discovery may advantage for car industry which need reflective light paints. *Science* magazine July 24, 2013 reported these findings. The research is important because the colour change is in this beetle is not due to biological reason but physical and hence we can replicate it with ease. Commonly when light hit a surface the rays may absorb or reflect or scatter and produce ;colour, but in the case of jewel beetle the color is produce by rearranging the five, six and seven sided cells themselves and produce yellow, green and red colors. Really it is an astonishing discovery and need to appreciate the researchers. This kind of cell may simulate liquid crystals which has free surface with cone like structure called "Cholesteric". The finding shows that these cells are nothing but chitin molecules—a polysaccharide. Now, the secret is going to commercialize due to its simplicity in reproduction and low cost of production. Its commercial value resides not only in automobile industry but paint industry also demands to produce paints which change its colour automatically as and when the viewers change his angle of view. Hence same colour may produce different colour effects, a single paint having multi colour effects.

Bird feathers produce color through structure similar to beer foam

According to Yale University the brightest colors in nature are produced by nanostructures with a structure similar to sponge or beer foam. The colour in nature is generally produced by pigments. But the bright blue colured in many birds are producing colour is because of the nanostructure and not due to the pigments. It appears as sponge with bubbles like structure under the electron microscope. Researchers compare this colour producing nano-particles with materials undergoing phase separation, like carbon-dioxide bubbles that form when a top is popped off a bubble drink. The researcher claims that the color producing in the feather is very similar to the phase separation. Water bubbles form in the protein rich soup inside the living cell, which later replaced by air as the feather is growing. This secret may be reproducing to make a new form of optical materials in the lab.

Now it's not just Spiderman that can scale the Empire State Building

Physicists all over the world found the formula for a Spiderman suit. Recently we came to know how spider and geckos climb walls, hang from ceilings without expenditure more energy and effort, but it is till doubtful whether this secret of natural adhesive can apply to Spiderman like activities. Researcher from various institute concluded that the secret behind the adhesive ability of geckos and spider is the van der Waals forces which held the molecules together and providing amazing adhesive power to the creature. It is also came to know that the tiny hairs on feet of spiders' attract to the molecules of surfaces, even very smooth glassy surface, and keep them steady. This secret take a leap by some researchers in the field of biomimcry by producing human suit with a series of adhesive force that is sufficient to hold the body against wall on which he is to climbing and can easily be detached. Nanotechnology can produce Carbon nanotube which can be used to develop nano-molecular hooks and loops and it may function like microscopic Velcro. This attachable and detachable adhesive force can be incorporated with van der Waals forces and capillary suction force. This new discovery can be applied in many field like space exploration, defense, preparing gloves and shoes for window cleaner of skyscrapers. Another advantage of this adhesive is that it is self cleaning and not requiring any cleaning agent and man power. It is also weather resistant and not clogs during the humid and hot weather; hence it will not tear and wear and can be used even in the deeper art of the sea.

Team Building Robotic Fin For Submarines

Bluegill sunfish (*Lepomis macrochirus*),is a freshwater fish also know as bream or brim or copper nose. IT is called so because the presence of blue edge on gill racks. The swimming motion of this fish fantastic and attracted many biomimcry experts to study in details. By inspiring from freshwater fish engineers are now preparing mechanical fin that can propel robotic submarines. This submarine can be used to map the underwater world and searching the hidden treasure in the ocean better than ever and even more important it can be used in military works. The attachment of AUV's will perform the underwater marine ship work better than today's machine. The researcher copies the secret from the bluegill fish because it cannot drag back during its forward motion. Even human cannot do this during the breast stroke because he felt backward dragging during his swimming.

Scientists find that squid beak is both hard and soft, a material that engineers want to copy

The maintenance of sharp and hard in the case of squids is a matter of research for biomimcry scientists. The squid sharpen and keep it hard without harm the body himself is amazing. We know that, the sharp beak of the squid, Humboldt, is one of the stiffest and hardest organic materials known. Biologists, Scientist of marine science and engineers are very interested I finding the secret of sharpening the beak of squids into knife like appearance without tearing into pieces. The researcher revealed that the key factor to the squid beak lies in the gradations of stiffness. The tip is stiff and the base is 100 times more compliant, allowing it to blend with surrounding tissue but it only works when the base of the beak is wet. When the base is dry it also become stiff as the tip. With one swift motion Humboldt squids, or Dosidicus gigas, are able to injure a fish.

New molecule can tangle up DNA for more than 2 weeks

Researcher at University of Texas at Austin, created a molecule can remain itself inside the DNA double helix sequence. This molecule can stay there for about 16 days before the DNA liberates itself. This kind of research can pave the way to create medicine that can directly enter them DNA and work. This kind of drugs a promising development in the field of genomic drug therapy for cancer or HIV, which inject viral DNA directly into the body's DNA. This drug molecule actually slides between the rungs of the DNA. It can creep between the rungs forward and backwards like a snake. The most important property of this molecule is that it cannot dislocate form DNA easily. Unlike other drugs used for HIV this new molecule can scan the entire body and attack wherever the DNA of the HIV is present and silence them one by one even in the early stage of infection. Present day drugs for HIV are used in the later stage of the disease so curing become impossible and death is the only result. Thanks to the DNA double helix structure and Watson and Crick for its discovery.

Researchers develop new self-training gene prediction program for fungi

Finding the gens in DNA is a tedious process. Software is now available to predict genes in DNA sample. Recently Georgia Institute of Technology produced a computer program to predict genes in the DNA sequences of fungi. Fungi are important for human health and industries. This knowledge can be used to produce new therapeutic drugs. Prediction of gene can also help to identify critical targets for vaccination and therapeutic intervention giant's pathogenic fungi.

Intones contain branching point sites, which are non-coding regions of DNA, located between exons. Before this invention predicting the exon-intron structure didn't search for branch point sites, but the present one did it well. The new version of eukaryotic genome self-training software program was developed by Borodovsky and his colleagues and proposed that fungal genes are more complex than other eukaryotes.

The gene finder is now called GeneMark.hmm-ES (BP), are available online, free for academic use. Borodovsky developed the first version of Gene Mark in 1993. In 1995, this program was used to find genes in the first completely sequenced genomes of bacteria and archea. The GeneMark.hmm-ES (BP) only requires the genome sequence. The program uses Hidden Markov Model to pinpoint the boundaries between exons and introns and intergenic regions. Dinucleotide guanine-thymine (abbreviated GT) is the starting sequence of most introns and end with the dinucleotide adenine-guanine (abbreviated AG). But, finding these sequences is not sufficient to confirm the presence of an intron.

The proof is in the tree bark

A study found that in the bark of trees across the northeastern United States contain chlorinated flame retardant Dechlorane Plus. The highest concentrations of it was estimated near the Niagara Falls, N.Y., factory where this chemical is produced. The study shows that the tree bark can be used as an indicator of chemicals of various kinds depending on the availability of the chemical in the air and soil in the vicinity; this in turn depends on the source of the chemical like factories. The bark is rich with fats and porous hence it imbibes the airborne chemicals very easily. More over the sampling from the bark did not harm the plant itself. The studies outside of the Great Lakes area also prove some good facts about this kind indication. OxyChem (Occidental Petroleum Corp.) Identifies the high concentration of DP is near the factory where the chemical is produced. The study also confirmed that DP Concentrations in tree bark is many times more in the nearby areas of factory as compared to the distant tree barks. Researchers also used tree bark as an indicator of brominated flame retardants at northeastern U.S. Locations. As DP the brominated flame also found more in the bark of tree present near the factories as compared to the distant one.

DP is used as a flame retardant in wiring and electrical cables and other products. The DP obtained from tree bark may be permanent solution for pollution free DP application in various industrial products.

An unmanned aerial vehicle that uses wind power like a bird—pure genius

Queensland University of Technology student Wesam Al Sabban designed an unmanned aerial vehicle (UAV), which was powered by the sun and wind and named it as Green Falcon II. Actually bird inspired its shape to design the aeroplan but here bird inspired to use air to design the Green Falcon II. The bird use only minimum energy to steer in the air and wind actually cause to change its direction. The researcher designed the Green Falcon II to forecast solar intensity and wind pattern. This kind of aerial unmanned vehicle is cheaper as it is powered by solar energy and fly like wind. This design was presented at 63rd iENA International Trade Fair, Nuremberg, Germany. As the Green Falcon II is a zero-emissions UAV and capable of round-the-clock service it will assist with disaster relief, 3D mine mapping, power lines inspection, and similar uses.

Acute artificial compound eyes

For the last many decades researcher found many useful secret that can be copied for many benefits in insects. Many researchers are working on ultra thin imaging system on the basis of insect compound eye. Hyperacuity principle of insect eye has now been successfully incorporated in a technical model. Each facet or omatidium picks up apportion of the entire object and then combine all the images to produce the image of the entire object is the mode vision in insect. This omatidia are spread on hemi arch, hence it can view a wide angle but the precision id very poor. This property make the insect very precise maneuvers and are able to do so because of the principle of hyperacuity Scientists are now trying to copy this imaging system in artificial eye and they hope that once it is achieved can incorporate in the eye of blind individual and can able to see as common man.

CHAPTER-9

Some Access point to Biomimicry

Biomimicry Institute

AskNature (http://www.asknature.org) retrieved on 12ᵗʰ Dec.2013

AskNature is the online inspiration source for the Biomimicry community. Think of it as your home habitat—whether you're a biologist who wants to share what you know about an amazing organism, or a designer, architect, engineer, or chemist looking for planet-friendly solutions. AskNature is where biology and design cross-pollinate, so bio-inspired breakthroughs can be born. Thanks to sponsors like Autodesk, AskNature is a free, open source project, built by the community and for the community. Our goal is to connect innovative minds with life's best ideas, and in the process, inspire technologies that create conditions conducive to life. To accomplish this, we're doing something that's has never been done—organizing the world's biological literature by function. What you'll see on the site today is a starter culture of ideas—biological blueprints and strategies, bio-inspired products and design sketches, and biomimics you can talk to and collaborate with. Over the next few months, this genetic pool of ideas will grow as we receive natural history information from our partner, Encyclopedia of Life. Our social web will also grow, beginning with tapping into thousands of solution seekers who are part of WiserEarth's global network. Luckily, we live on a wildly diverse planet surrounded by genius, and now there's one site where you can celebrate, learn from, and even conserve that genius. So please, come meet your mentors, get involved, and be part of the design revolution inspired by nature.

The Biomimicry Database

A prototype of the Biomimicry Database (a project of the Rocky Mountain Institute and the Biomimicry Guild) is available at http://database.biomimicry.org/. The database provides a mechanism of capturing and linking many types of data relating to Biomimicry, including:

1. Challenges
2. Strategies
3. Organisms
4. People
5. Citations
6. Products

A key feature of the database is the ability to define new taxonomies and ontologies as our understanding of how to structure information evolves.

Extensive help is available at http://database. biomimicry.org/db_intro_help.html (there is a link to the help file on the main database page).

Useful-websites

http://www.asknature.org/

Ask Nature is a library of biomimicry precepts compiled the Biomimicry Institute (with the assistance of IDEO) to help designers quickly and easily identify applicable natural principals.

www.biomimicry.net/

Biomimicry contains both a consultancy and a non-profit approach to emerging discipline that studies nature's best ideas and then imitates these designs and processes to solve human problems.

http://biomimicryeuropa.org/

This Biomimicry site provides news, cases and project samples; it aims to contribute to an alternative developmental route for modern civilization.

http://bioinspired.sinet.ca/

Bio Inspired provides newsletters, e-magazines, event s schedule and useful links about Bio-Inspired-Design.

www.biomimicrynews.com/

Biomimicry News archives engineering solutions gleaned from similar systems developed in nature.

www.biomimicryneo.org/
Biomimicry NEO is for business people and designers who are interested in networking and putting biomimicry to work at every design table.

http://bx.businessweek.com/biomimicry/news
Business Week's column, Biomimicry, enlists cases that show how businesses could be enhanced by imitating nature's creations.

http://www.biomimicry.info/index
Biomimicry Info provides information and ideas about biomimicry to be used by educators.

www.itconversations.com/shows/detail241.html
IT Conversations offers audio streaming and transcripts of a 30-minute presentation by Janine Benyus.

www.scidev.net/News/index.cfm?fuseaction=printarticle&itemid=1656&la
The Science & Development Network offers an article on how African termites give clues to the design of energy efficient buildings that adapt to a changing climate.

Websites for teachers

Video

Great video from TED by Janine Benyus—(23 minutes)—college http://www.ted.com/talks/janine_benyus_shares_nature_s_designs.html

CBS news 3 minutes intro video—elementary—high school http://www.cbsnews.com/video/watch/?id=5576995n

Janine Benyus (4 minute)—adult explanation of biomimicry http://www.bigpicture.tv/videos/watch/45fbc6d3e

Biomimicry in Space—European Space Agency (5 minutes) http://www.youtube.com/watch?v=3FYMRH3XVlo

Biomimicry and Evolution—For High School or college http://www.youtube.com/watch?v=JnBkbaFsZOY&feature=related

1.5 minute introduction to Biomimicry—good for middle school and high school students http://www.youtube.com/watch?v=BiMZYdVLqME&feature=related

Biomimicry video for presentation—2.5 minutes—David Suzuki and Janine Benyus from Bullfrog Film http://www.youtube.com/watch?v=6O4GsXyRE58&feature=related

Links

Biomimicry Institute—Great Site with Resources for Teachers
http://www.biomimicryinstitute.org/

AskNature.com—Part of the Biomimicry Institute—where biologists and designers cross pollinate

Biomimicry taxonomy—1,200 existing biometric examples
http://www.asknature.org/

15 Examples of biomimicry
http://brainz.org/15-coolest-cases-biomimicry/

Great explanation of biomimicry from an amazing book: World Changing
http://www.worldchanging.com/archives/003625.html

European biomimicry site
http://www.biomimicryeuropa.org/

Websites for Projects

Research existing examples of biomimicry
http://depts.washington.edu/natmap/education/protocols/14_biomimicry_student.html

Curriculum ideas involving biomimicry
http://www.biomimicry.info/Curriculum

Biomimicry contest with great links for research
http://www.kidsciencechallenge.com/

Curriculum ideas

From (http://www.biomimicry.info/Curriculum)

Biomimicry has the potential for integration into many disciplines and at many levels of teaching. On a basic exploration of the wonder of nature in the elementary school years; through integrated projects in environmental science, biology, and art classrooms in high school; to architecture, design and business schools (Eddy, J, 2005). Biomimicry combines lessons in the basics of ecology and biology while at the same time inspiring creativity and solution based thinking. As Zenobia Barlow, Director of the Center for Ecoliteracy points out, "learning thrives when it's centered on real-world projects" (Jenson, 2002, p. 6). In this section I will introduce two lesson plans that I have used involving biomimicry in the high school classroom (More resources can be found in resources). These are to serve as samples that can be used or modified. Certainly not all teachers or students are expected to know all the answers ahead of time. These are thinking exercises and open-ended. It is a powerful lesson when the teachers can let go of being the experts and let the students find the answers on their own (Barlow as cited in Jenson, 2002.) Like the examples above, this is certainly not an exhaustive list of ideas but only a representation of two very different ways to integrate the concepts into teaching.

Brainstorming from nature's amazing design: an exploration of artifacts

Unit concepts:

1. Animal and plant adaptations
2. Technology

Learning Objective: By having students use all their senses and their knowledge about artifacts from nature, students will recognize the amazing adaptations and design plans that are in ordinary objects. Students will use creative teamwork to come up with original ideas for biomimicry and therefore further develop an understanding of the concept.

Materials/prep: A set of artifacts from nature, one for every 2-4 students. If possible set the room up in a circle. Examples: Animal vertebrae, pine cone, butterfly, barnacle shell, abalone shell, egg shell, seed pods, crab claw, etc.

Lesson Format: Teacher begins with one artifact and asking students to brainstorm on the many jobs of this object and how it is designed to accomplish its job. Then the teacher explains biomimicry and asks the students if they can think of any application for the mentioned design problems we have in our lives. Students are then paired/grouped and given an unique artifact for each group to discuss in a similar manner with their group members. Teacher should circulate in order to help students with questions about less familiar artifacts, ask thought provoking questions and find out what the students are thinking. Then the class comes back together and each group (or volunteers, depending on time) will share their ideas with the rest of the class.

Assessment: Primary assessment occurs as teacher circulates among the brainstorming groups. Teacher can help individuals with clarification at this point. Final assessment comes when students present their findings to the class.

EXAMPLE: A deer vertebrae is designed to be protection, but also needs to allow for access of nerves in and out; It is also support of body and a connection point for muscles; it needs to have great articulation to be able to move in many ways; it is also a used for storing minerals, it is built of natural materials at body temperature. We could be inspired for building robot parts with such multi-functionality; we could also be inspired to create molds for products out of life friendly materials (and not heat, beat and treat it, or have unwanted waste left over); could we make a chair that can supply this much support but also be moldable and moveable to our position or mood.

Green city design project

A working knowledge of wide variety of ecosystem is very essential for the successful practicing of the environmental engineering. An engineer can understand abiut energy flow, nutrient cycle, chemistry and dynamics of liquids just by studying the ecosystem of lakes. Similarly one can understand biodiversity, portioning of light and how to interact different living things by studying the day to day activity of a rain forest. Decay and transformation of bio-energy can be better understood by studying this rain forest. By studying the different ecosystem like rain forest, tropical forest, coniferous forest, desert community, and aquatic habitat one can understand a lot of life variations and thir interaction patterns and cooperative life behaviors, which is essential to copy many ideas and secret of nature for the designing and production of biomimetics designing and process. Biomimetics designing, process and technology will helps us to a sustainable development and a long lasting biodiversity.

Unit concepts: (I use this project as a culminating activity to integrate units learned throughout the year).

1. Urbanization and transportation
2. Population growth · Biomes
3. Water use and watershed
4. Adaptations
5. Energy
6. Land management
7. Waste management

Learning Objective: Students will design a city using sustainable principals. Students have to realize the complexity of city and overlapping economy, environmental aand sociological needs. Students also practice to know the local problems and then correlate this aspect to the global scenario. For example challenges and solutions may be different for Miami verses Chicago.

Materials/prep: Large paper (butcher paper or poster boards) and colored markers Access to internet

Lesson Format: Students are put in groups of 3-4. I open with a dramatic introduction: "A natural calamity destructs the city totally and you have been called for replanting the city from the debris". Then each flock of students is given a city and placed the following questions: Find out 1) History of the area: Local climate, topography of the area and biome factors. Including anthropogenic factor 2). Then ask to do research on one plant in that an area. Ask the question why do this plant is highly adapted to this area? How could you use some of these ideas in your city plan? 3) Similarly do research on one of the animal in that area. How this species is well suited in that area? Then assess yourself which type of inspiration you derived from this study to set up the city as previously. 4). Also not forget to include the source of energy, waste management, and drinking water supply methods etc to include in your study.

Time: Three 50 minute classes or homework and a double block. If students have selected their area they can divide up research tasks for step one (either in the first class period or for homework). Divide the students into separate group for different duties like a group assign searching the map of the city, another group will look up the method of adaptation of plants and n animals in that locality, next group assign to do research on adaptation of local animals and plants to suit the local climatic conditions. Now in class discuss all the questions placed above and prepare a diagram based on their ideas.

Assessment: The group of students displays the city plan and other groups ask questions and draw a conclusion finally.

EXAMPLE: As an example, a group of Student selected a city from New Delhi, India. The students performed a detailed study of this city and found that it is desert area. They selected a thorny cactus and camel as the organisms for their inspiration. They find that the camel has many desert adaptations. Camel use its hump to store fats, when it is on long distance travel trough hot, dry, windy desert, the fat metabolize and water is forming, this water is sufficient to live for long distance travel. It may inspire new technique to store water in place were water scarcity is extreme. The camel protects its nostrils by a flap of skin for preventing the sweep of sands during wind, which is common in desert are. It may inspire to make new innovative nose flaps during desert sojourn. The thick pad of skin present under the foot spread while it walking through the hot, thick sandy desert, hence the foot cannot go deep in the sand and help to protect the foot from unbearable temperature of the desert. This may inspire new innovation idea for designing foot wears. Cactus also become an inspiration in the city to use solar energy, this energy can be used for heating purpose of water and other applications. Back up wind farm and biomass generation plant also designed based on the inspiration. Kangaroo rat is another inspiring animal in the desert environment. It makes burrow and homes are built with thick stone/ adobe walls or partial earth homes to maintain cooler temperatures without as much energy hungry air conditioning. Overhanging eves are used to keep midday and summer sun from heating home through windows. Also inspired by the kangaroo rat all water is conserved and reused as much as possible. Water in homes is on a grey water separation system in which water used for cleaning (sinks, showers, and washers) is recycled and used in garden and home plants. Gardens use xeriscaping for drought-tolerant, native plants. Therefore they need little to no watering. Residents are encouraged to compost food scraps and create natural amendments for their gardens with low organic desert soil. Local farms or home gardens use drip irrigation at night. There is a light rail system around town and safe bike paths are built throughout the city. There are some shopping districts which are pedestrian only. There is a rail stops nearby, and if people must drive the parking structure has many floors to keep cars shaded and even the top has a solar paneled roof to both provide surface generation but also shade. Apartments are located near and above shops so that many people can live and shop in one location. The city is become an ideal model for recycling system.

Ecosystem Website project & Niche Reflection

When learning about concepts, terminology, around ecology it helps to have a place to be intimate with in order to apply the ideas. Applying it to the local ecosystems is one way, becoming familiar with another, especially one far away that we have always wanted to know more about. Students pick an ecosystem from anywhere in the world and research a dozen organisms that live there.

They must find out about their niche, in other words what adaptations do they have to: live well here? Find food? Escape becoming food? Benefit from interrelations with other organisms? In choosing organisms they create a food web and web of connections. Given the non-linear format of this report, a website is an excellent way to present the material.

Again in discussion and reflection of the material can elicit wonder for the adaptations they learn and can be tied to a biomimicry brainstorming session.

Adaptation Auction—Game

This activity can be done in the classroom or outdoors. 6th-12th grade Note: Very fun, and often silly.

1. Divide the group into 4
2. Select 4 organisms and 4 habitats where they live. *(For Example: desert, tidepool, tundra, & redwood forest; and lizard, egret, crab, woodrat)*
3. Have the groups brainstorm on what adaptations their particular organism has that makes it very well adapted to its environment. Then share these with the entire group.

The challenge will be that the organisms may now be asked to survive in a new habitat. If these two organisms were put to the test—how would they do? But first, there is an opportunity to adapt new traits.

4. The entire group brainstorms their favorite adaptations that they have heard of in nature and they are all listed on a board for the group to see.
5. Each group is given 1000 points (dollars?) to spend in the auction. Open up the floor and move through the list you have created. Groups can bid on adaptations that they want. When the auction is over these new organisms are asked to plead their case as to why they would be the best survivors in the various ecosystems. You can have groups debate, act-out, do an "interpretive dance," etc. Afterwards (or throughout) you can discuss some pretty amazing adaptations and our

appreciation for what the various organisms that have them. This is a great introduction to the concept of biomimicry. Think of all the amazing ideas that are already out there for how to live, survive and thrive. Ask the students how we could use some of these great ideas to help out with products/needs in our own lives. We take this same inspiration to create technologies and materials which use nature as a guide.

Books on Biomimcry (http://www.amazon.com)

Biomimicry: Innovation Inspired by Nature by Janine M. Benyus

Biomimicry: Inventions Inspired by Nature by Dora Lee and Margot Thompson

Biomimicry for Optimization, Control, and Automation by Kevin M. Passino

The Mind of an Innovator: A Guide to Seeing Possibilities Where None Existed Before by Patricia Harmon

Thriving Beyond Sustainability: Pathways to a Resilient Society by Andres R. Edwards

ARCHITECTURE without architecture: Biomimicry design by Carlos Ginatta

The Sustainability Revolution: Portrait of a Paradigm Shift by Andres R. Edwards

Natural Capitalism: Creating the Next Industrial Revolution by Paul Hawken, L. Hunter Lovins and Amory B. Lovins

Cradle to Cradle: Remaking the Way We Make Things by William McDonough and Michael Braungart

Biomimetics: Biologically Inspired Technologies by Yoseph Bar-Cohen

Biomimicry as a metaphor for Perfect integration in sustainability: Nature, Biomimicry, Perfect integration, Sustainability by Asha Nilani Liyanage

Bulletproof Feathers: How Science Uses Nature's Secrets to Design Cutting-Edge Technology by Robert Allen

Biomimetics: Nature-Based Innovation by Yoseph Bar-Cohen

The Gecko's Foot: Bio—Inspiration: Engineering New Materials from Nature by Peter Forbes

The Ecology of Commerce Revised Edition: A Declaration of Sustainability (Collins Business Essentials) by Paul Hawken

Cats' Paws and Catapults: Mechanical Worlds of Nature and People by Steven Vogel

Thinking in Systems: A Primer by Donella H. Meadows

Biophilic Design: The Theory, Science and Practice of Bringing Buildings to Life by Nikos A. Salingaros

The ultimate flattery: learning from nature through biomimicry.(House & Home): An article from: E by Starre Vartan

Bioinspiration and Biomimicry in Chemistry by Gerhard Swiegers

Bio-ID4S: Biomimicry in Industrial Design for Sustainability: An Integrated Teaching-and-Learning Method by Carlos Alberto Montana Hoyos

Biomimicry: Architecture and Design by Ilaria Mazzoleni

Designing Tall Buildings: Structure as Architecture by Mark P. Sarkisian

Knowing the Creator Through His Creation: The Divine Gift of Biomimicry by Jim Darrach

Design For Life by Sim Van der Ryn

Photonic Structures Inspired by Nature (Springer Theses) by Mathias Kolle

Handbook of Bioinspired Algorithms and Applications (Chapman & Hall/CRC Computer & Information Science Series) by Stephan Olariu and Albert Y. Zomaya

Ultra-Low Power Bioelectronics: Fundamentals, Biomedical Applications, and Bio-Inspired Systems by Rahul Sarpeshkar

Biologically Inspired Robotics by Yunhui Liu and Dong Sun

Bioengineered and Bioinspired Systems (Proceedings of Spie) by Angel Rodriguez-Vazquez, Derek Abbott and Ricardo Carmona

Evolutionary and Bio-inspired Computation: Theory and Applications (Proceedings of Spie) by Misty Blowers and Alex F. Sisti

Designs Patterns & Textures ; for Creative Inspiration by Natalia Ray—Kindle eBook

Biomimetics—Materials, Structures and Processes: Examples, Ideas and Case Studies (Biological and Medical Physics, Biomedical Engineering) by Petra Gruber, Dietmar Bruckner, Christian Hellmich and Heinz-Bodo Schmiedmayer.

FURTHER READING

1. Shaohua Chen and Martin Ravallion, The developing world is poorer than we thought, but no less successful in the fight against poverty, World Bank, August 2008
2. 2007 Human Development Report (HDR), United Nations Development Program, November 27, 2007, p.25.
3. *Ibid.*
4. Today, over 22,000 children died around the world from this web site. (Note that the statistic cited uses children as those under the age of five. If it was say 6, or 7, the numbers would be even higher).
5. 2007 Human Development Report (HDR),
6. Millennium Development Goals Report 2007.
7. The State of the World's Children, 1999, UNICEF.
8. State of the World, Issue 287—Feb 1997, *New Internationalist*
9. 2007 Human Development Report (HDR), United Nations Development Program, November 27, 2007, p.25.
10. 2006 United Nations Human Development Report, pp.6, 7, 35
11. State of the World's Children, 2005, UNICEF
12. 2007 Human Development Report (HDR), United Nations Development Program, November 27, 2007, p.25

13. Millennium Development Goals Report 2007
14. *Ibid*, p.45.
15. *Ibid*, p.45
16. World Development Indicators 2008, World Bank, August 2008.
17. Millennium Development Goals Report 2007, p.44.
18. World Bank Key Development Data & Statistics, World Bank, accessed March 3, 2008.
19. World Bank Key Development Data & Statistics, World Bank, accessed March 3, 2008.
20. Trade Data, World Bank Data & Statistics, accessed March 3, 2008.
21. Eileen Alt Powell, Some 600,000 join millionaire ranks in 2004, *Associate Press*, June 9, 2005
22. Based on World Bank data (accessed March 3, 2008) as Total debts of the developing world in 2006: $2.7 trillion.
23. Top 200: The Rise of Corporate Global Power, by Sarah Anderson and John Cavanagh, Institute for Policy Studies, November 2000
24. Log cabin to White House? Not any more, *The Observer*, April 28, 2002.
25. Debt—The facts, Issue 312—May 1999, *New Internationalist*.
26. 1999 Human Development Report, *United Nations Development Programme* poverty-facts-and-stats. htm—fact26.
27. *Ibid.*
28. *World Resources Institute* Pilot Analysis of Global Ecosystems, February 2001, (in the Food Feed and Fiber section). Note, that despite the food production rate being better than population

growth rate, there is still so much hunger around the world.

29. The Scorecard on Globalization 1980-2000: Twenty Years of Diminished Progress, by Mark Weisbrot, Dean Baker, Egor Kraev and Judy Chen, *Center for Economic Policy and Research*, August 2001.

30. Maude Barlow, Water as Commodity—The Wrong Prescription, *The Institute for Food and Development Policy*, Backgrounder, Summer 2001, Vol. 7, No. 3

31. The state of human development, United Nations Human Development Report 1998, Chapter 1, p.37).

32. Otten A 2000 *Diploma Thesis* University of Ulm.

33. Vogel G. (1996): Manual of the special vegetables structure. Eugen Ulmer, Stuttgart: 1127th

34. Brodie,1975:http://database.portal.modwest. com/item.php?table=organism&id=1134.

35. Villavicencio,2002:http://database.portal.modwest. com/item.php?table=organism&id=1089

36. Vogel, K.P. 1996. Energy production from forages. J. Soil Water Conserv. 51:137-139.

37. Yu HH, Kim YH, Kil BS, Kim KJ, Jeong SI, You YO. 2003. Chemical composition and antibacterial activity of essential oil of Artemisia iwayomogi, Planta Med. 2003 Dec; 69(12):1159-62.

38. F. S. Nakayama, S. H. Vinyard, P. Chow, D. S. Bajwa, J. A. Youngquist, J. H. Muehl and A. M. Krzysik[c]. 2001. Guayule as a wood preservative, Industrial Crops and Products Volume 14, Issue 2, September 2001, Pages 105-111.

39. Maatooq *et al.*, (1996)http://database.portal.
modwest.com/item.php?table=organism&id=1115.

40. White. N.A, Hallett.P.D, Debbie Feeney,
Palfreyman. J.W, Karl Ritz. 2000. Changes to water
repellence of soil caused by the growth of white-rot
fungi: studies using a novel microcosm system,
FEMS Microbiology Letters 184 (2000) 73^77.

41. Ilan Greenberg, "Butterflies Show Path to Cooler
Chips," *Wired News*, http://wired-vig.wired.
com/news/technology/0,1282,10163,00.html.

42. Robert Kunzig, "The Beat Goes On," *Discover*,
January 2000.

43. Kurt Kleiner, `Fields of genes, *New Scientist,* 16
August 1997.

44. Phil Gates, *Wild Technology*, p. 54.

45. Peter M. Narins, "Acoustics: In a Fly's Ear,"
Nature 410, 2001, pp. 644-645.

46. Dr.Hanaslı Gur, "Bionic, Is To Copy Nature
"(Bionics Copies Nature), Science et Vie,
trans.: Science and Technology (Science and
Technology), TUBITAK Publishings, July 1985,
p. 21.

47. Erica Klarreich, "Good vibrations," *Nature
Science Update*, April 3, 2001.

48. Kevin Bonsor, "How Snakebots will Work,"
Howstuffworks; http://www.howstuffworks.com/
snakebot.htm.

49. Hinton, HE; Jarman, GM. 1972. Physiological
color change in the Hercules beetle. Nature. 238:
160-161.

50. Rassart, M; Colomer, J-F; Tabarrant, T; Vigneron,
JP. 2008. Diffractive hygrochromic effect in the

cuticle of the hercules beetle Dynastes hercules. New Journal of Physics. 10(033014): 14 pp.

51. Kim JH; Moon JH; Lee S-Y; Park J. 2010. Biologically inspired humidity sensor based on three-dimensional photonic crystals. Applied Physics Letters. 97: 103701-1-102701.

52. Frank Saunders *et al* 2011 *Bioinspir. Biomim.* **6** 016001).

53. A. J. Myrick and T C Baker 2011 *Bioinspir. Biomim.* **6** 016002).

54. A. Jusufi *et al* 2010 *Bioinspir. Biomim.* **5** 045001.

55. *Zsuzsa \'Akos et al. 2010 Bioinspir. Biomim. 5 045003.*

56. Murat Akçakaya and Arye Nehorai 2010 *Bioinspir. Biomim.* 5 046003.

57. Wang Zhang, Di Zhang, Tongxiang Fan, Jian Ding, Jiajun Gu, Qixin Guo and Hiroshi Ogawa. 2006. Biomimetic zinc oxide replica with structural color using butterfly (Ideopsis similis) wings as templates, Bioinspir. Biomim. *1 89.*

58. J D Davis, S F Barrett, C H G Wright and M Wilcox 2009. A bio-inspired apposition compound eye machine vision sensor system, *Bioinspir. Biomim.* **4** 046002.\

59. Demont, E. (Personal communication). Biology Professor, St. Francis Xavier University, Antigonish, NS. (2003).

60. Gosline J. M., Guerette P. A., Ortlepp C. S. & Savage K. N. The Mechanical Design of Spider Silks: From Fibroin Sequence to Mechanical Function. The Journal of Experimental Biology 202, 3295-3303 (1999).

61. Benyus, Janine M. Biomimicry: Innovation Inspired by Nature. Morrow, New York (1997).

62. Vollrath F. Strength and structure of spiders' silks. J Biotechnol. 2000;74:67-83.

63. Rising A, Nimmervoll H, Grip S, Fernandez-Arias A, Storckenfeldt E, Knight DP, *et al*. Spider silk proteins—mechanical property and gene sequence. Zoolog Sci. 2005;22:273-281.

64. Xu M, Lewis RV. Structure of a protein superfiber: spider dragline silk. Proc Natl Acad Sci USA. 1990;87:7120-7124

65. van Beek JD, Hess S, Vollrath F, Meier BH. The molecular structure of spider dragline silk: folding and orientation of the protein backbone. Proc Natl Acad Sci USA. 2002;99:10266-10271.

66. Simmons AH, Michal CA, Jelinski LW. Molecular orientation and two-component nature of the crystalline fraction of spider dragline silk. Science. 1996;271:84-87.

67. Lewis RV. Spider silk: Ancient ideas for new biomaterials. Chem Rev. 2006;106:3762-3774.

68. Sponner A, Vater W, Rommerskirch W, Vollrath F, Unger E, Grosse F, *et al*. The conserved C-termini contribute to the properties of spider silk fibroins. Biochem Biophys Res Commun. 2005;338:897-902.

69. Sponner A, Unger E, Grosse F, Weisshart K. Conserved C-termini of Spidroins are secreted by the major ampullate glands and retained in the silk thread. Biomacromolecules. 2004;5:840-845.

70. Huemmerich D, Helsen CW, Quedzuweit S, Oschmann J, Rudolph R, Scheibel T. Primary structure elements of spider dragline silks

and their contribution to protein solubility. Biochemistry. 2004;43:13604-13612

71. Motriuk-Smith D, Smith A, Hayashi CY, Lewis RV. Analysis of the conserved N-terminal domains in major ampullate spider silk proteins. Biomacromolecules. 2005;6:3152-3159.

72. Stephens, Thomas (2007-01-04). "How a Swiss invention hooked the world".

73. McSweeney, Thomas J.; Stephanie Raha (August 1999). Better to Light One Candle: The Christophers' Three Minutes a Day: Millennial Edition. Continuum International Publishing Group. pp. 55.

74. 71 "Heat-seeking vipers may help with U.S. defense, UT Austin researcher finds," On Campus, vol.28, no.08.

75. Peter Weiss, "Soaking Up Rays," Science News, August 4, 2001.

76. *Ibid*

77. *Ibid*

78. *Ibid*

80. Parker, A. R., "Water capture by a desert beetle," Nature 414, 2001, pp. 33-34.

81. Parker, 2001

82. *Ibid*

83. Ann Marie Cunningham, "Clothes That Change Color, ScienCentral.Inc" www.sciencentral.com.

84. Ilan Greenberg, "Butterflies Show Path to Cooler Chips," Wired News, http://wired-vig.wired.com/news/technology/0,1282,10163,00.html.

85. Robert Kunzig, "The Beat Goes On," Discover, January 2000.

86. Kurt Kleiner "The Internet strikes back," New Scientist, May 24, 1997.

48. Phil Gates, Wild Technology, 1998, p. 54.

87. SWAT'z new?—fly that's setting the hearing world abuzz", NIDCD, February 13, 2003.

88. Peter M. Narins, "Acoustics: In a Fly's Ear," Nature 410, 2001, pp. 644-645.

89. "Biyonik, Dogayı Kopya Etmektir" (Bionics Copies Nature), Science et Vie, trans.: Dr.Hanaslı Gur, Bilim ve Teknik (Science and Technology), TUBITAK Publishings, July 1985, p. 21.

90. Erica Klarreich, "Good vibrations," Nature Science Update, April 3, 2001.

91. *Ibid*

92. *Ibid*

93. *Ibid*

94. *Ibid*

95. K. A. Justice 2005 J. Neurophiol. **93** 2233-9.

96. A. J. Myrick and T C Baker 2011 Bioinspir. Biomim. **6** 016002).

97. Frank Saunders *et al* 2011 Bioinspir. Biomim. **6** 016001).

98. A. Jusufi *et al* 2010 Bioinspir. Biomim. **5** 045001.

99. Zsuzsa Ákos *et al* 2010 Bioinspir. Biomim. **5** 045003).

100. J.D. Davis *et al* 2009 Bioinspir. Biomim. **4** 046002.

101. Demont, E. (Personal communication). Biology Professor, St. Francis Xavier University, Antigonish, NS. (2003).

102. Gosline J. M., Guerette P. A., Ortlepp C. S. & Savage K. N. The Mechanical Design of Spider

Silks: From Fibroin Sequence to Mechanical Function. The Journal of Experimental Biology 202, 3295-3303 (1999).

103. Benyus, Janine M. Biomimicry: Innovation Inspired by Nature. Morrow, New York (1997).

104. Hu X, Vasanthavada K, Kohler K, McNary S, Moore AM, Vierra CA. Molecular mechanisms of spider silk. Cell Mol Life Sci. 2006;63:1986-1999.

105. Castillo-Davis CI, Mekhedov SL, Hartl DL, Koonin EV, Kondrashov FA. Selection for short introns in highly expressed genes. Nat Genet. 2002;31:415-418.

106. Kaplan D, Adams WW, Farmer B, Viney C. Silk polymers: material science and biotechnology. 1st ed. Washington DC: ACS Symposium Series; 1993.

107. Fraser RD, MacRae TP. Conformation in Fibrous Proteins. 1st ed. New York: Academic Press; 1973.

108. Gosline JM, Guerette PA, Ortlepp CS, Savage KN. The mechanical design of spider silks: From fibroin sequence to mechanical function. J Exp Biol. 1999;202:3295-3303.

109. 74. Kenney JM, Knight D, Wise MJ, Vollrath F. Amyloidogenic nature of spider silk. Eur J Biochem. 2002;269:4159-4163. [PubMed]

110. Slotta U, Hess S, Spiess K, Stromer T, Serpell L, Scheibel T. Spider silk and amyloid fibrils: A structural comparison. Macromol Biosci. 2007;7:183-188. [PubMed].

111. Hu X, Vasanthavada K, Kohler K, McNary S, Moore AM, Vierra CA. Molecular

mechanisms of spider silk. Cell Mol Life Sci. 2006;63:1986-1999.

112. Castillo-Davis CI, Mekhedov SL, Hartl DL, Koonin EV, Kondrashov FA. Selection for short introns in highly expressed genes. Nat Genet. 2002;31:415-418.

113. Kaplan D, Adams WW, Farmer B, Viney C. Silk polymers: material science and biotechnology. 1st ed. Washington DC: ACS Symposium Series; 1993.

114 Fraser RD, MacRae TP. Conformation in Fibrous Proteins. 1st ed. New York: Academic Press; 1973.

115. Gosline JM, Guerette PA, Ortlepp CS, Savage KN. The mechanical design of spider silks: From fibroin sequence to mechanical function. J Exp Biol. 1999;202:3295-3303.

116. Gerritsen VB. An airbus could tiptoe on spider silk. Protein Spotlight. 2000;24:1-2.

117. Kaplan D, Adams WW, Farmer B, Viney C. Silk polymers: material science and biotechnology. 1st ed. Washington DC: ACS Symposium Series; 1993.

118. Fraser RD, MacRae TP. Conformation in Fibrous Proteins. 1st ed. New York: Academic Press; 1973.

119. Vollrath F. Strength and structure of spiders' silks. J Biotechnol. 2000;74:67-83. [PubMed]

120. Nentwig W. Why do only certain insects escape from a spider's web? Oecologica. 1982;53:412-417.

121. Zschokke S. The influence of the auxiliary spiral on the capture spiral in Araneus

diadematus Clerck (Araneidae) Bull Br Arachnol Soc. 1993;9:167-173.

122. Gosline JM, DeMont EM, Denny MW. The structure and properties of spider silk. Endeavour. 1986;10:37-43.

123. Hu X, Yuan J, Wang X, Vasanthavada K, Falick AM, Jones PR, *et al.* Analysis of aqueous glue coating proteins on the silk fibers of the cob weaver, Latrodectus hesperus. Biochemistry. 2007;46:3294-3303. [PubMed]

124. Gao H, Yao H. Shape insensitive optimal adhesion of nanoscale fibrillar structures. Proc Natl Acad Sci USA. 2004;101:7851-7856. [PMC free article] [PubMed]

125. Arzt E, Gorb S, Spolenak R. From micro to nano contacts in biological attachment devices. Proc Natl Acad Sci USA. 2003;100:10603-10606. [PMC free article] [PubMed]

126. Townley MA, Tillinghast EK, Neefus CD. Changes in composition of spider orb web sticky droplets with starvation and web removal and synthesis of sticky droplet compounds. J Exp Biol. 2006;209:1463-1486. [PMC free article] [PubMed]

127. Vollrath F, Tillinghast EK. Glycoprotein glue beneath a spider web's aqueous coat. Naturwissenschaften. 2005;78:557-559.

128. Rising A, Nimmervoll H, Grip S, Fernandez-Arias A, Storckenfeldt E, Knight DP, *et al.* Spider silk proteins—mechanical property and gene sequence. Zoolog Sci. 2005;22:273-281. [PubMed]

129. Xu M, Lewis RV. Structure of a protein superfiber: spider dragline silk. Proc Natl Acad Sci USA. 1990;87:7120-7124. [PMC free article] [PubMed]

130. Lewis RV. Spider silk: Ancient ideas for new biomaterials. Chem Rev. 2006;106:3762-3774. [PubMed]

131. Hayashi CY, Lewis RV. Evidence from flagelliform silk cDNA for the structural basis of elasticity and modular nature of spider silks. J Mol Biol. 1998;275:773-784. [PubMed

132. Hayashi CY, Lewis RV. Spider flagelliform silk: Lessons in protein design, gene structure and molecular evolution. Bioessays. 2001;23:750-756. [PubMed]

133. van Beek JD, Hess S, Vollrath F, Meier BH. The molecular structure of spider dragline silk: folding and orientation of the protein backbone. Proc Natl Acad Sci USA. 2002;99:10266-10271. [PMC free article] [PubMed]

134. Simmons AH, Michal CA, Jelinski LW. Molecular orientation and two-component nature of the crystalline fraction of spider dragline silk. Science. 1996;271:84-87. [PubMed]

135. Gosline JM, Denny MW, DeMont EM. Spider silk as rubber. Nature. 1994;309:551-552.

136. Termonia Y. Monte Carlo diffusion model of polymer coagulation. Phys Rev Lett. 1994;72:3678-3681. [PubMed]

137. Becker N, Oroudjev E, Mutz S, Cleveland JP, Hansma PK, Hayashi CY, *et al.* Molecular nanosprings in spider capture-silk threads. Nat Mater. 2003;2:278-283. [PubMed]

138. Scheibel T. Protein fibers as performance proteins: new technologies and applications. Curr Opin Biotechnol. 2005;16:427-433. [PubMed]

139. Rising A, Hjälm G, Engström W, Johansson J. N-terminal nonrepetitive domain common to dragline, flagelliform and cylindriform spider silk proteins. Biomacromolecules. 2006;7:3120-3124. [PubMed]

140. Ittah S, Michaeli A, Goldblum A, Gat U. A model for the structure of the C-terminal domain of dragline spider silk and the role of its conserved cysteine. Biomacromolecules. 2007;8:2768-2773. [PubMed]

141. Sponner A, Vater W, Rommerskirch W, Vollrath F, Unger E, Grosse F, *et al.* The conserved C-termini contribute to the properties of spider silk fibroins. Biochem Biophys Res Commun. 2005;338:897-902. [PubMed]

142. Sponner A, Unger E, Grosse F, Weisshart K. Conserved C-termini of Spidroins are secreted by the major ampullate glands and retained in the silk thread. Biomacromolecules. 2004;5:840-845. [PubMed]

143. Huemmerich D, Helsen CW, Quedzuweit S, Oschmann J, Rudolph R, Scheibel T. Primary structure elements of spider dragline silks and their contribution to protein solubility. Biochemistry. 2004;43:13604-13612. [PubMed]

144. Hu X, Vasanthavada K, Kohler K, McNary S, Moore AM, Vierra CA. Molecular mechanisms of spider silk. Cell Mol Life Sci. 2006;63:1986-1999. [PubMed]

145. Motriuk-Smith D, Smith A, Hayashi CY, Lewis RV. Analysis of the conserved N-terminal domains in major ampullate spider silk proteins. Biomacromolecules. 2005;6:3152-3159. [PubMed]

146. Ayoub NA, Garb JE, Tinghitella RM, Collin MA, Hayashi CY. Blueprint for a high-performance biomaterial: full-length spider dragline silk genes. PLoS ONE. 2007;2:514.

147. Castillo-Davis CI, Mekhedov SL, Hartl DL, Koonin EV, Kondrashov FA. Selection for short introns in highly expressed genes. Nat Genet. 2002;31:415-418. [PubMed]

149. Exler JH, Hummerich D, Scheibel T. The amphiphilic properties of spider silks are important for spinning. Angew Chem Int Ed Engl. 2007;46:3559-3562. [PubMed]

150. Hermanson KD, Huemmerich D, Scheibel T, Bausch AR. Engineered Microcapsules Fabricated from Reconstituted Spider Silk. Advanced Materials. 2007;19:1810-1815.

151. Jin HJ, Kaplan DL. Mechanism of silk processing in insects and spiders. Nature. 2003;424:1057-1061. [PubMed]

152. Vollrath F, Knight DP. Liquid crystalline spinning of spider silk. Nature. 2001;410:541-548. [PubMed]

153. Riekel C, Bränden C, Craig C, Ferrero C, Heidelbach F, Müller M. Aspects of X-ray diffraction on single spider fibers. Int J Biol Macromol. 1999;24:179-186. [PubMed]

154. Gosline JM, Guerette PA, Ortlepp CS, Savage KN. The mechanical design of spider silks:

From fibroin sequence to mechanical function. J Exp Biol. 1999;202:3295-3303. [PubMed]

155. Kubik S. High-performance fibers from spider silk. Angew Chem Int Ed Engl. 2002;41:2721-2723. [PubMed]

156. Hayashi CY, Shipley NH, Lewis RV. Hypotheses that correlate the sequence, structure and mechanical properties of spider silk proteins. Int J Biol Macromol. 1999;24:271-275. [PubMed]

157. Rammensee S, Huemmerich D, Hermanson KD, Scheibel T, Bausch A. Rheological characterisation of recombinant spider silk nanofiber networks. Appl Phys A. 2006;82:261-264.

158. Dicko C, Kenney JM, Knight D, Vollrath F. Transition to a beta-sheet-rich structure in spidroin in vitro: The effects of pH and cations. Biochemistry. 2004;43:14080-14087. [PubMed]

159. Hijirida DH, Do KG, Michal C, Wong S, Zax D, Jelinski LW. 13C NMR of Nephila clavipes major ampullate silk gland. Biophys J. 1996;71:3442-3447. [PMC free article] [PubMed]

160. SenGupta S, Scheibel T. Folding, self-assembly and conformational switches of proteins. In: Zbilut JP, Scheibel T, editors. Protein folding and misfolding. New York: Nova Publishers; 2007. pp. 1-34.

161. Scheibel T. Spider silks: Recombinant synthesis, assembly, spinning and engineering of synthetic proteins. Microb Cell Fact. 2004;3:14. [PMC free article] [PubMed]

162. Ko FK, Jovicic J. Modeling of mechanical properties and structural design of spider web. Biomacromolecules. 2004;5:780-785. [PubMed]

163. Vendrely C, Scheibel T. Biotechnological production of spider-silk proteins enables new applications. Macromol Biosci. 2007;7:401-409. [PubMed]

164. Emile O, Le Floch A, Vollrath F. Biopolymers: Shape memory in spider draglines. Nature. 2006;440:621. [PubMed]

165. Emile O, Le Floch A, Vollrath F. Time-resolved torsional relaxation of spider draglines by an optical technique. Phys Rev Lett. 2007;98:167402. [PubMed]

166. Liu Y, Shao Z, Vollrath F. Relationships between supercontraction and mechanical properties of spider silk. Nat Mater. 2005;4:901-905. [PubMed]

167. Perez Rigueiro J, Elices M, Guinea GV. Controled supercontraction tailors the tensile behaviour of spider silk. Polymer. 2003;44:3733-3736.

168. Shao Z, Vollrath F, Sirichaisit J, Young RJ. Analysis of spider silk in native and supercontracted states using raman spectroscopy. Polymer. 1999;40:2493-2500.

169. Yang Z. Supercontraction and backbone dynamics in spider silk: C-12 and H-2 NMR studies. J Am Chem Soc. 2000;122:9019-9025.

170. Vollrath F, Madsen B, Shao Z. The effect of spinning conditions on the mechanics of a spider's dragline silk. Proc Biol Sci. 2001;268:2339-2346. [PMC free article] [PubMed]

171. Wilding MA, Hearle J. Fiber structure. In: Salamone JC, editor. Polymeric materials encyclopedia. Vol. 11. Bota Raton: CRC; 1996. pp. 8307-8322.

172. Shao Z, Vollrath F. Surprising strength of silkworm silk. Nature. 2002;418:741. [PubMed]

173. Arcidiacono S, Mello C, Kaplan D, Cheley S, Bayley H. Purification and characterization of recombinant spider silk expressed in Escherichia coli. Appl Microbiol Biotechnol. 1998;49:31-38. [PubMed]

174. Fahnestock SR, Bedzyk LA. Production of synthetic spider dragline silk protein in Pichia pastoris. Appl Microbiol Biotechnol. 1997;47:33-39. [PubMed]

175. Scheller J, Gührs KH, Grosse F, Conrad U. Production of spider silk proteins in tobacco and potato. Nat Biotechnol. 2001;19:573-577. [PubMed]

176. Trivedi BP. Lab spins artificial spider silk, paving the way to new materials. 2002. http://news.nationalgeographic.com/news/2002/01/0117_020117TVspidermammals.html.

177. Lazaris A, Arcidiacono S, Huang Y, Zhou JF, Duguay F, Chretien N, et al. Spider silk fibers spun from soluble recombinant silk produced in mammalian cells. Science. 2002;295:472-476. [PubMed]

178. Miao Y, Zhang Y, Nakagaki K, Zhao T, Zhao A, Meng Y, et al. Expression of spider flagelliform silk protein in Bombyx mori cell line by a novel Bac-to-Bac/BmNPV baculovirus

expression system. Appl Microbiol Biotechnol. 2006;71:192-199. [PubMed]

179. Huemmerich D, Scheibel T, Vollrath F, Cohen S, Gat U, Ittah S. Novel assembly properties of recombinant spider dragline silk proteins. Curr Biol. 2004;14:2070-2074. [PubMed]

180. Padgett KA, Sorge JA. Creating seamless junctions independent of restriction sites in PCR cloning. Gene. 1996;168:31-35. [PubMed]

181. Schmidt M, Römer L, Strehle M, Scheibel T. Conquering isoleucine auxotrophy of Escherichia coli BLR(DE3) to recombinantly produce spider silk proteins in minimal media, Biotechnol Lett. 2007 Nov;29(11):1741-4.

182. India rules hill city 'illegal' bbc.co.uk, 19 January 2011 Last updated at 00:57 ET.

183. UPDATE 1-India ministry sets terms to consider Lavasa approval reuters.com, Tue Jan 18, 2011 7:58am EST.

184. Biomimicry: Architecture That Imitates Life harvardmagazine.com, September-October 2009.

185. Lavasa Corporation Ltd: India's First Planned Hill City Deploys Portal Solution to Empower Employees; Increases Collaboration and Efficiency microsoft.com, 5/31/2010.

186. Howl of the hills downtoearth.org.in, by Nidhi Jamwal, Sep 15, 2008.

187. "Suzlon, Lavasa among named in India bribery scam-reports". *Reuters.* http://www.reuters.com/article/idUKSGE6AO03620101125.

188. "Environment Ministry asks Lavasa to halt project". *The Economic Times*. http://economictimes.indiatimes.com/news/news-by-industry/indl-goods-/-svs/construction/Environment-Ministry-asks-Lavasa-to-halt-project/articleshow/6994372.cms.

189. India's newest hill station builds for the future AFP news hosted by google.com, Sep 15, 2009.

190. HCC's Lavasa court hearing adjourned for 6 weeks reuters.com, Thu Jan 27, 2011 7:31am EST.

191. A Stop in India's Lavasa forbes.com, Dec. 20 2010.

192. "SHOWCAUSE NOTICE: JAIRAM ORDERS WORK TO STOP—Lavasa lands in trouble for flouting green laws". *The Economic Times*. November 27, 2010.

193. "Lavasa IPO may face delay: HCC Chairman". *Business Standard*. http://www.business-standard.com/india/news/lavasa-ipo-may-face-delay-hcc-chairman/118365/on.

194. Pawars no strangers to big land projects. http://www.dnaindia.com/mumbai/report_pawars-no-strangers-to-big-land-projects_1194953-all

195. Byatnal, Amruta (October 31, 2010). "Symbolic of luxury, Lavasa is built on irregularities". Pune. http://www.thehindu.com/news/national/article859868.ece. Retrieved February 21, 2011.

196. For four towns, see Discover Lavasa: Master Plan; A vision becomes reality Lavasa Official Site

1. For five towns, see Lavasa: Life in Full Lavasa Official Site (Page 4)
2. For seven hills, see Lavasa: Life in Full. Lavasa Official Site (page 2).

197. The hills are alive with the sound of controversy business-standard.com, September 7, 2010, 1:49 IST.
198. Thekaekara, Tarsh. "The great urban juggernaut". NewInternationalist. http://www.newint.org/columns/currents/2010/05/01/lavasa-indias-first-private-city/. Retrieved February 9, 2011.
199. For the golf course, see Faldo signs 'stunning' Indian course design project nickfaldo.com, 8th June 2009.
200. Ashokan.K.V and Pillai.M.M (2008). In silico characterization of silk fibroin protein using computatational tools and servers, *Asian Journal of experimental sciences*, 22(3)., 265-274

ABOUT THE AUTHOR

Ashokan Kannarath is presently working as a vice principal in a reputed college in Maharashtra. He completed his graduation and post-graduation in Calicut University, Kerala. He is a doctorate in cytopathology of aging and has 28 years of teaching experience in zoology. His research area includes natural science, bioinformatics and biotechnology. He has published 53 research articles in national and international journals, and 10 books including Mc Millan, India. He is a life member of various scientific bodies including association of Indian Gerontology, All India Science Congress, All India Association of Educational Research, Member of Editorial board Journal of "Science Education Review"–Melbourne Australia, Editorial board member of Integrated Publishing Association and National advisory board member: International Journal of Physiology, Institute of Medico-legal Publication, New Delhi, to mention a few. He is awarded "Quality and excellence in academia-2006", and recently "Best citizen of India" award 2013. He has guided many Ph. D works and thesis for graduate and postgraduate students. He is very much fond of biodiversity of Western ghat in India, especially rare medicinal plants and mammalian diversity. He has published many articles on biodiversity of mammals including lemurs in Madagascar Island.

This book is an outcome of his last many decades ardent observation of plants and animals in natural habitat. Janine M. Benyus, founder of Bioinformatics

Institute is the inspiration behind this book. In this book he explained a lot of natural process, secrets and ideas from animals and plants for the designing various applications ranging from Velcro-Zip fastener to highly sophisticated robots. He has also introduced some research areas in biomimicry and biomimicry in molecular level. The chapter on "some case studies in biomimcry" and "biomimicry access points" is one more feather to this book. For the researcher the "further reading" section and "index" to the text is most valuable one.

INDEX